BE YOUR BEST

CHANGE
MANAGER

. . . AND BEYOND

Peter Young

Q·LEARNING

For UK orders: please contact Bookpoint Ltd, 130 Milton Park, Abingdon, Oxon OX14 4SB.
Telephone: +44 (0) 1235 827720. Fax: +44 (0) 1235 400454. Lines are open 09.00–18.00, Monday
to Saturday, with a 24-hour message answering service. You can also order through our website
www.madaboutbooks.co.uk

British Library Cataloguing in Publication Data A catalogue record for this title is available from The
British Library.

This edition, first published in UK 2003 by Hodder Headline Plc, 338 Euston Road, London NW1 3BH

Copyright © 2003 Peter Young

Typeset by Servis Filmsetting Ltd, Manchester, England
Printed in Great Britain for Hodder & Stoughton Educational, a Division of Hodder Headline Plc, 338
Euston Road, London NW1 3BH by Cox & Wyman Ltd, Reading, Berkshire.

Impression number   10 9 8 7 6 5 4 3 2 1
Year   2007 2006 2005 2004 2003

Contents

Series Introduction

Perhaps you have had an idea, or wanted to achieve something, but known that you not only need some skills but also help with taking the risk and doing it for real. Maybe you have thought 'it is easy for him/her but not for me . . .'

This series is written for people who haven't got the time (or money) to attend a long training course or who are not lucky enough to be managed and mentored by a star in the field in which they want to succeed. These books will be 'back pocket' resources that will inspire and give practical tips that you can read up on and use in the next few minutes. They will also help you feel confident in taking skills that you already have into new situations at work, home and the community.

Lesley Gosling
Q. Learning

Introduction: Change Manager

This book addresses the needs of managers and leaders who wish to increase the probability that their planned change projects will achieve successful outcomes. In the business of change there are no guarantees; despite your best intentions, projects encounter resistance, or go off course. So what would it mean to find examples of 'best practice', and change your approach to implementing change? Neither in life nor in business does anyone have the option of *not* changing. The simple rule is: make it *easy* for other people to do what you want them to. In *Change Manager* you will learn how to make life easier both for yourself and for those will will be implementing your plans.

This book is built on the premise that change comes from shifting your point of view. Using this paradigm, Peter Young takes you through the applications and consequences of this way of thinking, and explains how you can be more effective in getting other people to join with you in realizing your vision.

Planning is vital. You are envisioning the world as you would like it. Visions that are rich in detail and well thought through will be compelling for others. Informing others is not about 'winging it' or 'it'll be all right on the night.' If you prepare the way for other people, they will accept your vision and want to be part of it. Then change becomes easy.

The most effective way of motivating people is to tell a story. We live in a storytelling culture: think about the obsession with news, gossip and media personalities; with Hollywood movies and the latest bestselling books. People are hooked on stories, so why not use stories to get your message across – to help others understand how things will be changing. People who buy into your story are far more likely to go along with your proposals.

Actually, once you look beneath the surface, you will probably recognize how this works, because you have already had a lifetime's experience of stories that change lives. It's just that you never noticed the principles before, because with good communication the *structure* is meant to stay in the background.

So learn how to create a vision that will persuade others, and how to structure your message using metaphors and stories that will motivate your team, your clients and your customers. By adjusting the way you communicate to others, you will be helping them change their way of understanding what needs to happen. And the result is not only that you have a united team, but that you also can deal far more effectively with any resistance or conflict you encounter.

Change Manager provides many real-life examples of people who have 'told their stories' and brought about significant changes in the world as a result. Now you can become your own success story.

Peter Young is an innovative thinker, who is fascinated by how people come to understand themselves and their lives through the 'models of the world' they develop, the metaphors they use, and the stories they tell themselves to explain what happens.

Peter studied Psychology at the University of Hull, and researched brain function and learning styles at the University of Adelaide. He also studied Drama at the Flinders University of South Australia, and has maintained a life-long interest in film and theatre, improvisation, plot-structure and storytelling.

He has worked as a management trainer, created training videos, and has written explanatory books on NVQs. He first encountered NLP in 1984, trained with John Seymour Associates, and worked for Ian McDermott of International Teaching Seminars. He has written numerous articles for *Rapport* (the magazine of the UK Association for Neuro-Linguistic Programming) and has given presentations at the ANLP Conferences. Since the mid-1990s Peter has been rethinking NLP, and his groundbreaking book *Understanding NLP: Metaphors and Patterns of Change*, published in 2001, is his account of a new model of change.

Prologue

You must *be* the change you wish to see in the world.

MAHATMA GANDHI

The only way to make sense out of change is to plunge into it, move with it, and join the dance.

ALAN WATTS

Change is a paradox. It offers great opportunities for learning more about yourself; and it frustrates your attempts to create a stable and predictable world. It tests your responses: do you resist or do you ignore change; do you try to balance opposing forces, or do you go with the flow of change? If you intend to perturb that flow and create change in other people, in groups, in organizations, or in the world, then you need to know how best to do it, and how best to deal with the consequences. People have been dealing with change, successfully and unsuccessfully, since time began. What seems certain is that there are no magic bullets, no short cuts or quick fixes that will guarantee that you will get what you want. What matters is how well you learn from experience.

In the process of planning and implementing a change project you will inevitably be changing yourself. It goes with the territory. As a change manager you will be facing many of the same problems and issues as your clients. You are acting as a role model for others. Your ability to influence others depends on how you personally deal with change. If you are being honest and authentic, they will copy you, and will be encouraged to then take greater responsibility for their own change processes in due course.

Simply imposing change on others is usually a waste of time. It creates resistance, resentment, even revenge, and you end up with the opposite of what you set out to achieve. Rather than trying to control or manipulate other people, a better strategy is to find ways of getting inside the other person's mind and finding out 'where they are coming from', or 'what makes them tick'. Because that is going to be different for different people, you need to know the range of variation. A good place to start is by finding out where *you* are coming from. You will need some personal discipline for exploring what goes on in your mind, what you believe, what you think, your attitudes and preferences. You do not need anyone else's permission for doing this, and you are always available for testing new ideas. Moreover, you can stop whenever you like. That is the challenge of this truly do-it-yourself book.

Planning and implementing change is not about applying rules such as: 'In situation X, follow process Y, and you will get result Z.' It just doesn't work like that. You are dealing with people who have their own beliefs, values, preferences, ideas, and they are not going to be easily shifted. Instead of offering techniques for 'applying' change by decree, the numerous exercises in this book are designed to stimulate your thinking about *how* you can change the way people perceive their reality – sometimes referred to as their 'mind-set.' (The word 'perceive' covers seeing, hearing, feeling and thinking.) When you find out how people create their 'model of reality' in their mind, you will have a better idea of how to communicate with them, and how to help them think in a more positive and resourceful way about changing.

Think of your job as making it easy for others to change. They will want to comply because your enthusiasm suggests it is worth doing, and they can see how it is in their best interests. One of the most effective ways of making change easy is to tell a story. Storytelling has been around since ancient times. It is still a favourite means of communication, and has become a major industry encompassing journalism, publishing, the media, television, movies from Hollywood and other film studios, and so on. People thrive on stories, and appear to have an insatiable appetite for them.

However, one of the beguiling aspects of good stories is that they draw you into their world, and you forget to pay attention to *how* they work. When you know what good storytellers are doing, you can use that skill to help motivate others with your vision of how things could be. Because the busy world is so much with you, you may find it hard to stand back and identify the patterns of change that run through your life. This book, therefore, provides an opportunity for noticing some of the patterns and stories that run beneath the surface of our society.

There is one particular pattern you will meet. It is very old, and many variations of it have appeared over the millennia. There are also numerous manifestations of this pattern in modern management texts, but in most cases only the surface details, not the underlying pattern, are revealed. I call this the Six Perceptual Positions Model, and you will find an explanation in Chapter 7 of how this fundamental pattern is derived. You will learn how to use it to develop your own techniques and processes for exploring change, and to structure the stories you will tell others.

Once you are familiar with this pattern, you will notice it everywhere! Consequently, here is a warning: a pattern is just a pattern. The fact that a pattern occurs widely does not mean that it is some kind of 'ultimate truth' or 'unifying theory' – these are also stories that you have for making sense of the world.

Stories, models and paradigms are all ways of sorting the mass of information we receive every moment. They also bias our perception so that we only see what we expect to see. But then, this is true of all human communication and understanding. Change, then, is about learning to perceive in different ways. The art lies in knowing what to pay attention to and that is probably something not immediately apparent. Therefore a major part of implementing change is teaching other people what they should be paying attention to, because that is probably something they are not already aware of.

Although the terms *change manager* and *change leader* are both used in this book, there is a significant difference between leading and managing. This difference becomes clear as the book unfolds. Change does not start with a committee, but within the visionary's mind, the person George Bernard Shaw refers to as 'the unreasonable man'. Therefore I am assuming that whatever label you apply to this role, essentially you have the imagination to envision how things could be different, the power and the opportunity for doing things differently, and the ability to communicate effectively to other people. There is no point in having a vision that cannot materialize. Neither is there any value in alienating the project team or the clients, so that they are unwilling to buy into that vision or engender resistance to the proposed changes to their status quo. Your job is to motivate other people sufficiently so that they will want to become part of your dream. This book is about how you do this.

CHAPTER 1
Changing

And when the woman saw that the tree was good for food, and that it was pleasant to the eyes, and a tree to be desired to make one wise, she took of the fruit thereof, and did eat, and gave also unto her husband with her; and he did eat.
And the eyes of them both were opened . . .

GENESIS 3: 6–7

If I have seen further it is by standing on the shoulders of giants.

ISAAC NEWTON

THE AWFUL TRUTH

Who is really good at creating change? Suppose you could model your behaviour on some outstanding examples: scientists, inventors, creative artists, diplomats, spiritual leaders, and so on. Imagine that you are able to find out what those people do or did – their specific behaviours, thoughts and supporting beliefs. What exactly do they do that enables them to achieve outstanding results? If you knew those secrets, then all you would have to do is adjust your behaviour so that you could be a great leader of change.

As you look into this, the awful truth dawns upon you that these people cannot actually explain how they do what they do. They often attribute their success to being enlightened, to luck, to coincidence. Some claim it derives from being in the right place at the right time, or from having the right parents or genes. Alas, it would be impossible to create these conditions yourself. So what are you going to do?

Sometimes it seems that the world has not actually changed that much over the last few thousand years: there are still many unhappy people arguing, fighting, dropping bombs, and developing new technologies for eliminating everyone who disagrees with them. Is it possible to create positive life-enhancing changes instead? Is it still the case that there is nothing new under the sun?

Theories about change have been exercising the human intellect for thousands of years. In that time there have been many explanations and stories about how change happens. Much of the recorded wisdom tells you *what* to do, but not necessarily *how* to do it. To find out how, you need to look beyond the actual words and discover the underlying patterns and principles of action suggested by those stories. However, modern wisdom warns that simply applying techniques straight out of a book reduces your chances of success. You need to think about how you can adapt and integrate the information into your own way of working. In that way, the wisdom becomes yours.

Here is the strategy: find out what these common patterns are; understand how they can be best used in implementing change; adapt and restate the ancient wisdom in today's language.

THE RATE OF CHANGE

Historically there may seem to be evidence for 'instant' changes, but changing how people think often takes a long time. For example, our understanding of genetics started with Gregor Mendel analysing peas in the mid-nineteenth century. A major shift came in the 1950s when the structure of DNA was elucidated. Dr Rosalind Franklin created the first photographs showing the helical nature of the DNA molecule. Standing on her shoulders, as it were, Crick and Watson saw the photos, figured out the structure and published their article in the science journal *Nature*. This led to the Genome Project, which is ongoing.

To avoid later regret and revision, take time to think through the consequences of technological change. Be prepared for the unforeseen results. For example:

> There is a ready market for stolen expensive cars. By making the cars more secure, the only way to steal them is to strike at the remaining point of vulnerability, which is when the driver has the key in their hand. Instead of stealing an empty car, thieves now use violence on the driver.

TWO DOMAINS OF CHANGE

Change takes place both 'out there' in the tangible and physical world, and 'in here' in the internal world of your mind, with all your memories, thoughts and ideas. The world appears both 'objective' and 'subjective.' A change project starts from the subjective, inside your imagination, and gradually works out into the reality of managing other people and organizing things in the world. Because change starts from within, you need to know how to transform your ideas and what you imagine the future will be like, into physical reality. How can you literally make your dreams come true? Effective change leaders share their dreams or visions with others, so that together they may bring them into existence. Doing that affects everyone concerned. Tim Smit, the creator of the Eden Project in Cornwall, England, says:

> No one has a monopoly on dreams, but only a rare few discover the alchemist's art of making them real. Making things real demands a commitment that goes way beyond what a busker can give; it requires a single-mindedness and determination to succeed that persuade others as much by the force of your conviction as by the idea itself.
>
> SMIT, 2001B:16

Tim Smit uses the word 'busking' to refer to his earlier pleasurable lifestyle, living on his wits and enjoying good company. Eventually, he realized, you have to face up to yourself. You are your own 'harshest critic', and you know that doing what is easy is no substitute for real thought and feeling.

The way the world is – the physical, technological, social environments – is an outcome of human thought and intervention. Wherever you are right now, take a moment to look around you. Everything you perceive was once an idea in some person's imagination. Electric lamps, computers, books and pens were ideas that someone transformed into the reality you now see, hear or feel. Few places are truly 'natural'. The landscape is 'artificial'; it has been fashioned by centuries of agriculture, mining and industry. People cut back the forests, grew crops, dug claypits, and built roads and houses.

What needs to change?

How often do you complain about things not working? It is easy to find fault with the way our society runs. Even bearing in mind that people are usually well-intentioned and doing their best, this is what you have ended up with! If you want to know what to change, it is simple. Notice anything you are dissatisfied with or that does not work. Think of something that currently annoys or frustrates you. Then ask yourself: 'What would be better?' Imagine an improved world, and then wonder: '*How* could I find a way of achieving that?' This is where knowledge and expertise are vital. Software developer Bob Gaskins, creator of PowerPoint, says:

> I'd grown up in the audiovisual business, and I had access to audiovisual marketing data, and I knew, in the early 80s that there [were] a thousand million presentation slides being made per year, just in America. And I also knew, because I had been all round the world trying to buy things, that the rest of the world also used presentation slides the same way. . . . But they were all made by hand. Almost nobody was using computers to do so. The reason was . . . that these first generation computers, like the Apple II and original IBM PC were completely unable to deal with graphics. . . . But it was clear to me that here was a huge application, worth billions of dollars a year, that could be done on computers as soon as there was a revolution in the kinds of computers that we had. . . . It took four years before PowerPoint

was actually ready to ship. By that time everybody was coming around to that point of view, and it became obvious that even so it was a hard sell at that time, because . . . I had to say to my investors, 'Now this software will not run on any existing personal computers. We are going to write off the entire installed base of personal computers. Anybody who wants to use our software will have to buy a new computer.'

GASKINS, 2002

Getting from the idea to the reality takes time – and much of that time will be taken up with persuading others that your idea is worthwhile. The way to influence others is to 'sell them the idea' so that they can see the future benefits for themselves. How to do this is covered in Chapter 3.

Dealing with the complexities of change

There are no simple ways of proceeding with complex issues. To begin to unscramble some of the complexity, we have developed useful 'rules of thumb' for 'What to do when X happens . . .'; and other general theories that help us understand what would be worth doing, or explain what happened.

THREE KINDS OF CHANGE

The I–R–T Change model differentiates three kinds of change. It is based on Bateson (1972), Anderson and Anderson (2001), and Young (2001).

Table 1.1 The I–R–T Change Model

Level *I–R–T*	*Anderson and Anderson*	*Bateson*
Level I **I** **Inform**	Developmental	*First Order, Type I Change.* New information lets us improve what we already have. Rearranging what is to make it more efficient, work better.
Level II **R** **Reform**	Transitional	*Second Order, Type II Change.* By re-forming what we have into something new, we can move to a new way of doing things.
Level III **T** **Transform**	Transformational	*Third Order, Type III Change.* Transforming means changing the way change happens. As part of the system that is changing, we are thinking differently.

I: Level I Inform/Developmental

🔄 Improve what already works.

🔄 Keep things operating smoothly and more efficiently.

Informing change is about making small changes or improvements as the result of new information, new processes, new technology. Although there is new information, the boundaries of the system stay the same. *Informing* provides a description of what is, and improves its state, structure or quality.

A Type I change rearranges what already exists inside the fixed boundaries, improves the quality, or the way things are done: How can we do this faster, cheaper, more effectively, take less time, reduce costs, and so on? Generally speaking you end up with 'more of the same'. You make more products, extend the range, expand into new areas, open new outlets, and so on. For example, a Type I change for the Eden Project is the building of the third biome, and extending the range of plants on display.

R: Level II Reform/Transitional

🔖 Do something different.

🔖 Move to a different way of being/doing/working.

Reforming change introduces movement, adds novelty, and crosses the boundaries, seeking targets, goals, objectives that are currently outside of the current system. The challenge is to imagine something different and strive towards it. *Reforming* means taking alternative views, finding new perspectives and new uses, keeping what works and losing what doesn't, and finding new ways of restructuring and combining things.

A Type II change gets you 'thinking outside of the box' by introducing new material, other points of view, doing things differently. Alternatively you could combine two previously separate concepts. This has already happened at the Eden Project. Tim Smit's background in the music business has led to making Eden one of the UK's leading live music performance venues. The location has also been used as a set for a *Bond* movie.

T: Level III Transform/Transformational

🔃 A new way of thinking.

🔃 Accept that there are alternative ways of understanding and explaining reality.

Transforming change means changing the way you are thinking, and getting a new understanding – a 'paradigm shift'. Learning is a transformative process; integrating new experiences that influence future behaviour and thinking. The challenge is to accept that *everything* will be different, and in unexpected ways. Transforming is not about tweaking an existing system. You are separate from the world, 'neutral' or 'objective'. You are part of the system that changes.

A Type III change is a learning experience which reframes or restructures what you know, so that things will never be the same again. For example, is the Eden Project about plants, or is it about education, the arts and entertainment? Tim Smit has already established the Foundation, 'a place to learn about the possibilities and wonders of the world', which makes the Eden Project a dynamic experience which is there to entertain, educate and challenge the visitor into thinking differently about the world they are a part of.

A brief explanation

You can't solve the problem with the same thinking that's creating the problem.

ALBERT EINSTEIN

The three types of change form a hierarchy. To get an overview of an issue, you must rise to a level above it, and let your thinking expand into a bigger space. We have sophisticated change models for the first two levels, Inform and Reform, which allow us to think at the level above. We can solve problems at the level of Transformation, because we can observe what happens from 'outside of the system', as it were. Traditionally, scientific investigators and experimenters perceive themselves as 'neutral observers' outside of the system they are investigating on the lower levels. However, you cannot observe how transformational change occurs, because you are unable to step further outside. Conceptualizing a Level IV (see Bateson, 1972) severely challenges the human mind. So with transformational change, you must acknowledge that you are within the system under study, and therefore unable to act objectively. The physicist Max Planck expands this idea: 'Science cannot solve the ultimate mystery of nature. And it is because, in the last analysis, we are part of the mystery we are trying to solve.'

CHANGING MIND-SETS

> At first people refuse to believe that a strange new thing can be done, then they begin to hope it can be done, then they see it can be done — then it is done and all the world wonders why it was not done centuries before.
>
> FRANCES HODGSON BURNETT

So *how* do you manage change? If not through direct control, then one option is to find out the optimum conditions for change to happen. There are already many interesting strategies and practical techniques of change. However, this book focuses on what goes on in the mind of the person dealing with different kinds of change. What makes change easy for some people and hard for others? What are the beliefs and attitudes of people who achieve success? How do they think about what they want? How do they work with others, and get them motivated and committed to the change project?

There are some important clues to be revealed by understanding how an individual perceives the world in their mind. How do they perceive 'reality'? What is their *mind-set*? (Other terms in use are: *mental models*, *worldviews*, *models of the world*, *models of reality*.) If someone has a mind-set that makes it hard for them to change, you might be able to help them change that particular mind-set so that they become more mentally flexible.

Some key factors in changing minds

◊ **A positive attitude**. 'Things will be different somehow. I don't know exactly what is going to happen, but I am ready for it.' Being ready means being in the best state – physically and mentally – for dealing with whatever happens.

◊ **The ability to communicate brilliantly to others**. This means listening as well as talking. Communicating is a two-way process, and works better when you are in rapport with the other person. It also means being able to see things from their point of view.

◊ **An open mind**. Accepting what happens. Being open means that you stay 'switched on' to what other people are offering you, in terms of the suggestions they make, the ideas they have about what they want to do, and so on. Accepting means acknowledging what is actually happening, even when it seems awful, rather than burying your head in the sand, or denying what is obvious to others.

🔖 **Having appropriate cognitive models** that enable you to perceive what is happening. For example, conflicts arise because the various parties are arguing at cross purposes. The models in this book offer a way of understanding how this occurs and what makes their positions different. The models also suggest what you can do to help people understand each other. This is covered in Chapters 7–9.

Cognitive models provide ways of integrating learning, so that you can adapt general principles for any particular issues.

An excellent way of promoting change is to become a role model of change for others. The better you can 'walk your talk' – be a living example of good change practice – the more you will inspire others to do the same. If you are willing to change, others will follow.

Are you ready to take the next step? Fortunately you have a built-in detector – ask yourself 'Am I ready?' and note your response. If you get a 'Yes, but . . .' or feel unsure, then something is not ready yet. If possible, find out what is still needed. Otherwise be willing to accept the level of readiness: 'This is how it is – for now.'

THE VISION

Tim Smit's first horticultural project, The Lost Gardens of Heligan, was based on instinct.

> I saw Heligan and decided instantly that I wanted to do it. Like a madman. Everything was a risk and it felt very vital. I was following my instincts, as usual, and became very attached emotionally. Of course, in hindsight people say, 'Oh what a clever idea' or whatever, but people don't realise that you were within weeks of bankruptcy and you had every chance of losing everything because you were going for it.
>
> SMIT, 2001A

A vision needs to inspire you to great things, and other people to join you. Involve others by telling them a story; good stories capture the imagination. Tim Smit influenced people to work with him when he told them that he wanted to build 'the eighth wonder of the world'. They were even willing to do this for no pay initially. That is some vision!

If this seems too big, a flight of fancy, take one step at a time. Find out how other people manage to do all of these things, and more. There is no shortage of excellence you can draw on.

PERSONAL CHALLENGES

A change project is often a personal transformation; you will never be the same again! You are acquiring further wisdom, creating new maps, and so developing a superior set of practical principles to follow. Instead of copying someone else's recipe, you are learning to cook. Well, this book will provide some recipes, but it will also explain the principles they are based on. Adapt them, and create your own feast!

You learn best when you are curious, ask questions, and actively seek answers – you will do this more effectively when you care about the changes you want to make. It means taking time to assimilate what you are learning: notice generalizations, make connections and find commonalities with other experiences. It is easy to glide through life, grazing on titbits of pleasure, riding the roller coaster of emotion, and fail completely to understand what *you* do to affect what happens in the world around. By accepting your responsibility for whatever happens, you 'own' the learning.

You also need to find out how other people learn. As a change manager, you need to be able to build rapport with other people, which means first finding out how they think, and how they prefer to do things. A major part of the task is aligning ways of thinking with your vision of how things could be. New, improved practices will be accepted once they have been shown to bring the benefits of greater customer satisfaction and loyalty, and a more rewarding future for everyone. When their own best interests have been acknowledged, people begin to take responsibility for caring about others.

There is much to do as you set out on another change journey. To cultivate your own learning, pay particular attention to any ideas in this book that challenge your present way of thinking. Notice any initial resistance, how you respond, how you overcome it. In this way you will develop your own theories for explaining how change works, and the better prepared you will be for whatever happens in the future.

CHAPTER 2
Modelling and Outcomes

There are two tragedies in life. One is not to get your heart's desire. The other is to get it.

GEORGE BERNARD SHAW, *MAN AND SUPERMAN*,
ACT IV

Immature poets imitate; mature poets steal; bad poets deface what they take, and good poets make it into something better.

T. S. ELIOT, *THE SACRED WOOD*

THE SHRINE OF PERSONALITY

We learn by mimicking other people's behaviour. It starts with our parents and peers, and continues throughout our lives. As children we just do it; later we pay attention to specific skills that we want to learn. To meet this need, there is a continual supply of books and videos which demonstrate the how-tos of, for example, the perfect golf swing, losing weight or painting in water colours.

You are more likely to learn *how* to do things when you engage with the person doing them. Developing a skill is more demanding than changing your hairstyle, or wearing the latest clothes. You have to see beyond superficial appearances. Understanding the principles of what you are doing comes from a meeting of minds; which is why you need the real person, not just a dummy. What motivates them to do that? What are they thinking? What makes them good at it? These are often difficult questions to answer, but that does not stop you wanting to find out. This chapter suggests some ways to elicit some of this information.

WHY BE BETTER?

People strive to improve themselves. Our notion of evolution implies that there is a 'betterness' to which we aspire. We also have a talent for being dissatisfied with our current lot. Comparing ourselves to those we perceive as superior, more charismatic, more innovative and more successful than ourselves, we endeavour to upgrade our own abilities. In a business world which thrives on competition, organizations strive to become market leaders by increasing market share. Profit is only one form of motivation; we want to live in a more cooperative and peaceful world, to achieve our desires, to be happy.

What needs to improve?

It is easy to overlook what you have already achieved. For example: good relationships; an understanding of the world and other people; the ability to organize events, speak a foreign language, or play golf. All such abilities are evidence of your resourcefulness, your own best practice. And there will still be other areas of life you want to improve:

- ✎ Your environment, the conditions in which you live and work.
- ✎ Your performance, what you do.
- ✎ Your competence, your flexibility and range of skills.
- ✎ Your motivation, enthusiasm and desire to be better at what you do.
- ✎ Your understanding, your ability to learn and develop ideas.
- ✎ Your being, becoming who you really are.

Personal improvement

Progress now

Take a moment to think about what is missing in your life right now. Be specific.

- ✎ What do you want *less* of?
- ✎ What do you want *more* of?

For example, less stress, fewer demands on your time? Or more interesting work, more challenges, more learning, or more leisure and pleasure? Wants vary at different stages of life – and at different times of the day.

Following this line of thinking, consider: 'If I had that, how would I be better?' Does 'better' mean you want to be a better person, or better at doing things? Are these different? Does 'being better' mean being better than other people? Do others have to perceive you as better than them? Or is this something that you alone know: 'I have my ways of being 'better' — and other people have theirs. Isn't it great we are all improving!'

> What would being better enable you to do that you can't do now?

> If you were better at that, what would happen as a result?

Your answers will probably be different each time you answer these questions. Record and date your responses; it could be extremely interesting looking back on them in the future.

What matters is how you are going to improve. One way is to identify key elements or patterns in what you already do, and then apply them in other contexts. The more you know about your talents, the easier it becomes to see what exactly it is that works. There are further exercises for getting to know yourself better in Chapter 4.

NOTICE WHAT ISN'T WORKING

People have a natural talent for judging what they do not like, for noticing what *is not* working. If you do nothing about it, you may merely try to apportion blame. A positive enthusiasm, on the other hand, may lead to innovation, to finding ways of improving things. The inventor, James Dyson said:

> I was using a vacuum cleaner one day, at home, which had a bag in it, a paper bag in it, and I found it wasn't giving me any suck. And then I opened it up, and discovered that the bag wasn't full at all. In fact it was a virtually new bag, but I did notice a layer of fine dust all around the inside of the bag. And I suddenly realised that the reason it wasn't sucking was that the air was supposed to pass through the bag, and the pores of the bag were becoming quickly clogged. . . . So I realised that if I could come up with a vacuum cleaner that didn't have a bag, or a bag-like filter, I could solve this problem of loss of suction. So that is what I set about to resolve.

DYSON, 1998

Problem-solving

In a problem-solving culture, managers pay more attention to what isn't working; they look for problems to solve and ask 'Who's to blame?' Problem-solving strives to reduce or remove the limitations, difficulties and destructive actions by others. If you know what you don't want, just do the opposite. If you are ever stuck for a change project, simply notice what doesn't work or really annoys you, or situations where you find yourself saying 'There has to be a better way!' And then vow to do something about it. This could keep you busy for a lifetime!

Progress now
Your favourite gripes

List some of your favourite gripes. Think about what annoys you, what makes you frustrated or even angry. Start with everyday occurrences. Saying: 'There should be . . .', 'If only they'd . . .', 'Why don't they . . . ?' or 'They ought to . . .' indicates an unmet need, an opportunity ripe for change. For example:

🔊 **Queuing** – at distribution outlets, on production lines, to get into exhibitions.

🔊 **Transport** – delays, cancellations, traffic jams, parking problems.

🔊 **Public squalor** – rubbish, graffiti, unsafe neighbourhoods.

🔊 **Attitudes** – surly staff, unhelpful assistants, poor service.

Apply this to yourself, by considering personal frustrations and challenges:

🔊 'I *ought* to be better at X.'

🔊 'I *should* be a better Y.'

What would these Xs and Ys be?

In this way you can create a list of the kinds of personal improvements you would like to achieve. It is OK to fantasize – imagination is the departure lounge for the flight into reality.

Another way of coming at this is to see the world from someone else's point of view. If you were doing their job, what would you imagine frustrates them? What would their gripes be?

Progress now

Reversing the polarity

Knowing what you *don't* want, consider: 'What do I want instead?' This sets you on a quest for positive improvements in yourself and in your professional environment. Clarify your desires by thinking about how you would like the rest of your life to pan out:

- What do you want personally?
- What do you want professionally?
- What do you want for your business, your organization?

Write down what it is you want. And then, for each want, consider:

- 'Do I know how to achieve that?'
- 'Do other people know how to achieve that?'

If you know it is feasible, but you do not yet have the know-how, then *benchmarking* and *modelling* provide possible solutions. If you do not know, then you will need to 'dream something up' – and this is covered by outcome setting.

BENCHMARKING AND ADOPTING BEST PRACTICE

The real essence of benchmarking are the words 'finding' and 'implementing' best practices. Find the best practices and then creatively implement those best practices to get the results that you want.

BOB CAMP, FORMER EXECUTIVE OF XEROX

Benchmarking is the study of best practice – wherever it is found – in an organizational or business *process*, and the transfer of that knowledge to your own situation. As models of excellence can be discovered in any field, you must search widely to find who does this process better than you currently do. The thinking is: 'Why invent it yourself if someone else has already made it work well?' However, some people believe that creative solutions must start with a blank sheet of paper, and that 'inventing' is superior to 'copying.' The 'reinventing the wheel' mind-set is likely to result in wasting resources. An important shift in thinking is that you are learning how to learn from others, in whichever business they are in. In practice, benchmarking is an ongoing learning process. Although considered 'a good thing,' little rigorous benchmarking is actually done; it is more disciplined than just thinking up good ideas and implementing them.

Benchmarking is conducted as a formal process of gathering detailed information. The primary focus is on the task. Analyse best practice in terms of the procedural, 'mechanical' aspects of how things are done. Pay less attention to the people doing those tasks, other than to ensure they have had adequate training and possess the appropriate attitude for performing successfully.

Be systematic. To know how you are improving, you need a baseline standard or benchmark against which you can measure progress. Get to know your baseline in detail by meticulously gathering data on every aspect of your current performance levels, practices and processes. Later you will be able to contrast this with anyone else's better practice. Complete analysis is vital for proper comparisons to be made.

A frame for learning

- Acknowledge that there is much to learn.

- Assume that everyone does something you could learn from.

- Set a clear goal. Identify the difference between where you are now and where you want to be. Ask: 'What do we need to do to achieve competitive advantage?'

- Adopt an attitude of 'There must be a better way' and diligently seek it out.

- Because benchmarking will have an impact across the organization, you need to communicate what is happening to everyone involved.

THE XEROX STORY

Xerox, the market leader in the photocopier business during the late 1970s, saw themselves as 'pioneers' with a 'monopoly' and were becoming complacent. Then Japanese companies starting selling products in the American marketplace at a price comparable to Xerox's unit manufacturing costs. To meet this challenge from the Japanese, Xerox committed to benchmarking in order to stay in the game. They decided to benchmark organizations who could teach them how to improve performance, and began liaising with the sportswear mail-order company L.L. Bean. Although this might seem perverse, the concern was a generic problem of how quickly items could be retrieved from the warehouse. Both organizations had to deal with types of materials very diverse in terms of shape, size and weight; both were very labour-intensive. The differences in performance were dramatic. L.L. Bean had nearly three times as many stock items, and their staff could handle four times as many items per day as Xerox. In their investigation, Xerox learned that instead of having items sorted by product line, L.L. Bean stocked the most frequently needed items closest to where the people worked, so that they were immediately available. Such is the difference between the logical viewpoint of keeping things together, and the practical view of the workers who had to retrieve them.

With hindsight, such common-sense changes seem obvious. Everyone at Xerox became engaged in the benchmarking process. By sending out 15–20 teams a year to other organizations to study alternative processes at first-hand, the Xerox teams came to own the knowledge and wisdom they were acquiring. As a result, the Xerox employees, from manager to workers on the product line, became more curious, began to seek out ways of improving every aspect of their work, not just the specific manufacturing techniques, and to learn from sources of excellence wherever they found them.

Getting to the essence

Transferring knowledge means applying the *essence* of what works to new situations. Gather plenty of information and analyse it to discover that essence – the general principles involved – by looking beneath the surface detail. Be careful when studying an organization in the same business, as your perception will probably be biased (the 'availability error' – see Chapter 10) and you may be less inquisitive because you think you understand what is happening.

Modelling expertise and excellence in others requires proven skill in the art. Therefore, before looking at the specific systems you want to copy, it might be more productive to develop your competence in a good modelling methodology. You also need to sort out authorization and any other legal problems. There are legitimate moral and legal sanctions against copying and industrial sabotage, and concerns about confidentiality. To get useful information you need others' agreement and cooperation. If you are in different businesses, sharing information is not normally seen as a threat; in the same business, it could be classified as 'market sensitive'.

If a competitor's performance is vastly superior, the transformative change you need could mean a radical restructuring. Instead of arbitrarily adjusting targets: 'We will do 10 per cent better next year', take a critical look at work processes and procedures, how the organization perceives its business. As most organizations have reduced their manufacturing costs to the minimum, and there is little quality difference between products, further changes may have to involve improving the productivity of administrative and office functions. Alternatively, rather than tweaking the present system, you may want to fundamentally rethink the kind of business you want to be in. At the end of Chapter 11 there are some examples of trends in society that you could heed, and of new ways in which you meet your customers' needs.

Resistance to benchmarking

All change projects encounter resistance. The first task is often to change attitudes, and that means starting with top management. Everyone advocating change needs to set an example for others. If you do not believe in what you are advocating or demonstrate your own willingness to change, why should anyone else be inspired? This is often the most difficult part of instigating change. Changing minds is challenging – and there are no quick-fix, sure-fire methods for achieving it.

Benchmarking is more likely to be accepted in cultures where people are flexible and open to change, rather than hung up on secrecy. Even so, it is common to find scepticism about adopting best practice from other industries. Some organizations have a chauvinistic attachment to their history, and take a perverse pride in the historical accidents that made them different from their competitors. They believe: 'We are unique.' When confronted by better practice they respond with '*We* didn't invent that' – implying 'Therefore it won't work for us!' Before adopting anything innovative, managers require proof that it will work for them.

Finding models of excellence

These will be in your business, and in other industries. The key piece of good practice you are looking for may come from anywhere. *Process* is more important than the *content*, so:

- Look beyond your usual range of competitors.
- Study the whole system: from upstream suppliers to downstream customers.
- Identify who is outstanding. It is better to study a few world-class companies in detail rather than a multitude of good organizations superficially.
- Get hard data on cost, quality, time lines and customer acceptance.

Here is James Dyson (2001) being interviewed by Libby Purves:

Purves: So what you basically did was you used cyclones . . . columns of air, a fluid technology, a sort of spiral of air to do the sucking job, rather than just vacuum?

Dyson: Yes. You see them outside saw mills. It's that sort of large, upside-down wine-bottle outside a saw mill. . . . We had to build one [for] our ball-barrow factory for collecting fine dust. I saw the technology then, and I suddenly thought, why don't we miniaturise this and use this in a vacuum cleaner? So I rushed home, ripped the bag off my cleaner and made a cardboard cyclone and got a swimming pool hose and it appeared to work. But the invention wasn't quite as simple as that because to actually collect fine dust is very, very difficult.

'It's not that simple!'

One of the main reasons people fail to reproduce best practice is that they think it is easy, and become overoptimistic and overconfident. Writing in the *Harvard Business Review*, management professors Szulanski and Winter (2002) comment:

They try to perfect an operation that's running nearly flawlessly, or they try to piece together different practices to create the perfect hybrid. Getting it right the second time . . . involves adjusting for overconfidence in your own abilities and imposing strict discipline on the process and the organization.

They recommend that a model of excellence should be copied exactly, and that you need to get comparable results before adopting the new way of doing things. The people who got it to work the first time have developed expertise because they 'have probably already encountered many of the problems you want to "fix".'

The business guru Sir John Harvey-Jones (1988) warns that when people set out to copy something exactly, they tend to 'improve' it because they think they know better. He suggests that what you should do is 'minimise the changes that are sought if the objective is to have the plant functioning reliably as quickly as possible'. However, an exact copy 'is almost impossible to build', especially if you are shifting across cultures, or because of the legislative, technological and environmental changes in society.

MODELLING

Modelling places greater emphasis on the *person* than on the process. You select people to model who consistently demonstrate personal excellence in what you would like to be able to do as well. Modelling is more than just copying the superficial aspects. The art lies in being able to elicit and replicate the essential elements of what that person *does*. It might seem easy to do that by observing their behaviour or by asking questions. However, there are so many aspects of their performance that you could pay attention to, and so much potential information available, that the task may become overwhelming – or never-ending. At some point, collecting even more information will not help. The art is in knowing when to stop, that what you have is 'good enough' to begin emulating their performance.

Asking questions can lead you astray. The person being modelled either cannot tell you because they do not know themselves – after all, they have been doing this for some time and no longer have to think about it – or you do not know how to interpret their verbal descriptions: 'Well, you have to be in the zone . . . .'.

Although you recognize the words they use to communicate their associations and meanings, the meaning you make of them will inevitably be different.

You know you can become better, but you cannot do this 'in theory' — you have to do it for real. Observe and copy your chosen role model's physiology, movement patterns and timing. Ask questions to elicit their procedures, strategies, rules, and how they know what to do in different circumstances, when things 'go wrong', when there are decisions to make. Gather information on their beliefs about causality, connections, associations, relationships, and so on. Test for the key elements of what produces their expert behaviour by trying out those things for yourself, and notice whether you can improve. Practising a new skill requires noticing what is not working yet, and what needs to be changed, tweaked or modified. Having reached one level of competence, you collect the next piece of information necessary for moving on. Modelling is essentially a process of successive approximation, of adding extra pieces until you get there. Once you have found out the 'differences that make a difference', make that skill your own by integrating those essential elements into your way of being and doing things.

Life-long modelling

Each of us grows up modelling those around us: parents, siblings, peers and teachers. In this way we acquire language and life skills. We match (and in our teenage years, mismatch) the behaviours, attitudes and values of our role models. Because we do this naturally, often without thinking about it, we indiscriminately pick up the good as well as the bad.

Progress now
Current influences

Who currently inspires you as a role model for mastery of change or for being skilled at implementing change in others? For whom would you make some sacrifice – travel a great distance, pay a great price – to be in the physical presence of? Make a list of all such people, and consider: What do they do that you wish to emulate?

Progress now

Who influences me?

When you think back over your life, which characters stand out as 'people who influenced me in some way'? These might be inspiring teachers, charismatic relatives or friends, or even fictional characters in books or movies. However long ago that first encounter, their influence continues to inspire you now.

Make a list of the people that you modelled in some way. Then consider:

- What qualities did they demonstrate that inspired you?
- How exactly did they influence you?
- How did your life change as a result?

Better understanding

Good modelling requires some understanding of your role model's mind-set: their thinking, beliefs, attitudes and so forth. In other words, to achieve a comparable performance, it helps to know 'where they are coming from', to emulate their personal 'operating system'. It is a delusion to assume other people think more or less as you do. They don't! The 'impossible' challenge is to get inside someone else's mind and find out what they are actually thinking. The skill is learning to interpret their verbal descriptions and your direct observations, and integrating that new material into your existing knowledge. Habits of perception often lead people to expect only certain kinds of information, and they miss anything out of the ordinary. To recognize the 'unexpected' you need a wide knowledge of models, theories, patterns and paradigms.

Although everyone has a unique worldview, there are common patterns to be found in our society. If your change projects are going to be effective, you need to know what these underlying patterns are. Chapter 1 introduced a basic change model; Chapter 7 provides an explicit model for moving through change.

OUTCOME SETTING

Both benchmarking and modelling adapt existing solutions or best practice. However, when there are no obvious examples available, you must create workable solutions in your imagination. Build upon your existing experience by combining old ideas in new ways. Innovation emerges from novel juxtapositions.

The following guidelines incorporate the best practice of those people who bring their imagined goals into reality. Use them to increase the likelihood of achieving your outcomes.

Practical goal setting

1   Think positively about what you want, rather than what you want to avoid. Outcomes stated negatively are more likely to produce exactly what you don't want! For example: 'Stopping smoking' draws attention to the smoking behaviour rather than what you would do instead.

2   Goals can be *general* or *specific*. General goals would be: 'We want to find a way of/invent a device for doing X.' 'I want to be better at communicating my needs.' General goals are useful when you are open to change, and for inspiring others who will then come up with the specific details. People interpret vague goals ('better standards') in their own way. Politicians often propose fine

sounding objectives (wiping out terrorism, cutting drug use, reducing global warming), but how to achieve them is unspecified and may be impossible.

3 Break down big outcomes into relatively short-term manageable sub-goals, that will give you small successes along the way. In this way everyone gets a sense of (partial) completion.

4 Establish a feedback system that lets you know you're on track to getting what you want. Build in flexibility: have contingency plans, alternatives for getting to your goal. Define an 'exit procedure' detailing the specific evidence that tells you when to stop. Set a deadline, after which this outcome becomes obsolete.

5 Specify the level of performance required. Some outcomes need only be 'good enough'. Excellence or perfection – such as zero defects – comes at a price.

6 Limit the number of goals for any particular team or group. In general, people are not good at multi-tasking (although women are allegedly better at it than men). Anything more than one goal at a time could potentially cause internal conflict, because unresolved goals may nag away at the back of the mind and be distracting.

7 Ensure that what you want is in keeping with your personal values, your moral and ethical beliefs. It is pointless achieving outcomes that you would not want to live with, are 'not really me,' or do not align with the identity of the organization.

8 Choose goals that create options, rather than close down choices. Life becomes more interesting when you have more possibilities for the future. A transformative change project should be interesting of itself, not hyped up. People should want to own the vision, be part of it.

9 A goal should benefit all of mankind – or, as the medical profession suggests, 'at least do no harm'. Think 'bigger' and choose outcomes that enhance humanity, rather than just you and your immediate customers.

10 The longer the duration of the project, the more the world's political and economic environment will change. Your original goal may become obsolete. World events are unpredictable; it is unwise to assume that conditions will persist for long periods.

11 Goals need to mesh with other people's projects, goals, outcomes. This is especially true for joint projects, such as building aircraft. You need to know what others (intra-organizationally, regionally, nationally and globally) are engaged in, especially if at some stage you will be combining your outputs. Ensure your shared computing systems, paperwork, documentation, measurement systems (metric/imperial) are compatible.

Revise your plans as you think these points through, and ensure that your outcome is:

(53)

   Desirable – you still want this;

- ↻ **Appropriate** – it is in keeping with your personality, ethics and lifestyle;
- ↻ **Ecologically sound** – you would feel comfortable if this actually happened;
- ↻ **Achievable** – it is possible to do this;
- ↻ **Worthwhile** – it adds value to human existence; and
- ↻ **Interesting** – there is more to be explored.

Finally, ask yourself: 'Am I ready for this?' Notice your internal response. If you feel unequivocally that you are ready now, then go right ahead. On the other hand, heed any niggling 'Yes, but . . .' feelings. What is not yet right? Can you really commit to this project? (Be honest!) Every objection needs to be cleared before going ahead.

Actually getting what you want is not a precise art. Setting outcomes is often an exercise of hope. You do not know precisely what will happen, but you can set up conditions to make your goal more likely to happen. Your quest is to find out the best conditions for transforming your vision into reality.

Creating a *vision* (see Chapter 3) has been far less documented. A vision is inspirational in that it is 'bigger' and takes you beyond your currently perceived boundaries.

CHAPTER 3
Vision

If you want to build a ship, then don't drum up men to gather wood, give orders, and divide the work. Rather, teach them to yearn for the far and endless sea.

ANTOINE DE SAINT-EXUPERY

When a goal is really good, it doesn't just belong to you. A transformation occurs, and you belong to it. It makes you proud and humble, both at the same time.

ROBBINS AND FINLEY, 2000: 45

BELIEVING IT WILL HAPPEN

Creators of great change strongly believe in what they are doing, and those beliefs affect everything they do. Most importantly, they believe in themselves, that they are worthy of undertaking projects that will fulfil them personally, and will benefit the world in general. Believing in yourself means that you have the determination and ability to see things through, and trust that you can deal with whatever happens along the way. The road to the success of the Eden Project was beset with challenges – raising money, flooding, landslips, making 90,000 tons of soil from waste material, and so on – but having created a shared vision, the project team were willing to work extremely hard to meet them.

Change is stressful and a change leader must be in good physical condition. Maintaining a good state through the ups and downs means having good time management because numerous other 'important' things will compete for your attention. However, taking time to think the project through in detail at this initial stage is critical to the success of the project. You need time to imagine consequences, foresee possible glitches, and explore options. You need to network and connect with your own and other people's relevant experiences.

56

TAKING RESPONSIBILITY

Only by believing that you personally can have a positive effect on the world, and by accepting responsibility for your own actions, will you be effective in creating changes. A positive mind-set offers open access to the unlimited resources there are available, although some people may need convincing of this truth. A useful conviction is that whatever you believe about the nature of the world, the universe and everything – you are going to be right! If people perceive themselves as 'victims' of circumstances or unknown forces, controlled by 'fate' or 'destiny', this becomes true for them and helping them change may become exceedingly difficult.

How you act depends upon how you believe the world works. If you subscribe to what is sometimes called the Scarcity Model – which assumes there are only limited resources available – then you may find your time taken up with ensuring that you get as much as possible, regardless of others' needs. If, on the other hand, you are inclined more towards an Abundance Model – which presupposes unlimited resources – you will naturally find yourself cooperating with others, as together you enhance human experience. Using a cake metaphor, the Scarcity Model says: 'There are only so many slices available, so I must ensure my slice is as big as possible'; whereas the Abundance Model has the attitude of: 'Let's bake a bigger cake.'

These beliefs are at the extremes of a continuum. Any individual, organization or society can move to any position along that continuum. For some issues, the mind-set will be oriented more towards Abundance, and people will act collaboratively; while for issues which people are less happy about, the orientation is towards Scarcity, with selfish attempts to manipulate others. As most change projects include other people, success is more likely if you cooperate with them and if you believe that what you want will offer benefits to all.

IMAGINING A VISION

And all I ask is a tall ship and a star to steer her by.

JOHN MASEFIELD, *SEA FEVER*

As soon as you think of a change you would like to make – such as improving the banking system, reclaiming derelict land, or perfecting a golf swing – your mind starts producing images, sounds, feelings and words, and the universe begins to change! Tim Smit says: 'I believe in the Tinkerbell theory, which is that if you believe in a great idea then it will exist.' (Tinkerbell is the fairy in J.M. Barrie's *Peter Pan*, whose existence depends on children believing in fairies.)

Part of your task is to identify the 'star' that will guide you and your team through a change project. This guiding star illuminates your vision and focuses action and effort towards its fulfilment. Therefore, it must be sufficiently motivating and powerful so that in times of confusion or doubt, you can refer to your guiding principles, and ensure that you get back on course. Having clear and meaningful guidelines means that people will be aligned in their actions, working together to achieve that positive shared vision.

PASSION

The process of goal setting often starts by moving away from a 'negative' perception of what is not working, towards what needs to be different. Every negative implies some kind of 'opposite', and it is from a range of 'opposites' that you must choose which alternative you are willing to embrace. This will be the one which has the greatest emotional impact, both on you, and on the other people involved.

Being emotionally engaged is an overriding aspect of achieving what you want. You have to care about what happens, perhaps feel passionately that this future comes true. Alternative futures must be worth changing for, or else people will not believe in them, and will thus lose interest. Ask: 'What's at stake?' Often it is the future of the company, and the jobs of those people working there. What is at stake at the Eden Project in Cornwall is partly a revitalization of the economy by creating jobs, finding ways of using derelict land, and encouraging people to have something they can be proud of.

When you have created a proposal for the change project, check whether you really care about achieving this goal. If not, why are you spending time and energy on it? If you are going to 'sell' this notion to other people, and if you are not convinced, then why should they be?

If you are taking on someone else's change project, you need to be convinced that they are fully committed to its implementation. If this is not obvious, then you may need to do some gentle probing, asking questions about what is at stake, how much they care, and so forth. They may need help in clarifying their objectives, uncovering their value system and in acknowledging their emotional investment in their business. They may not call this 'emotional' or use the term 'passion', but refer to 'trust' or 'commitment' as the fundamental qualities that keep them in business. No matter. Businesses without passion tend not to last long.

CREATING THE VISION

> Change is an act of the imagination. Until the imagination is engaged, no important change can occur.
>
> ROBBINS AND FINLEY, 1977

Realizing a desired future requires imagination. Creating a vision means thinking on a bigger scale and in far more detail. The richer your mental landscape, the more powerfully you can communicate your ideas to others. Your great idea has to encompass all the complex ideas, plans, consequences, and so on, that will enable you and your project team to bring it into reality.

A vision offers a lively ongoing alternative reality. Tim Smit's first plan was to restore a greenhouse at his Lost Gardens of Heligan project to show useful plants from around the world, because 'Plants bring people together. Using plants is something that we all have in common.' He then calculated that such a greenhouse would cover several hectares and began looking for more space. Driving through Cornwall's industrial landscape the Eden Project came together: the 'greenhouse' could be in an old clay pit. The vision was growing. At each stage more people, excited by Tim's vision, got involved in this unique project.

Progress Now

Enriching your vision

Expand your thinking and create a believable and robust world that is sufficiently rich in detail so that you can answer any questions about how it works. You will need answers to the following questions:

Who? Questions about the project team

Knowing who is involved provides some notion of the available resources, talents and skills.

- Who is involved in this project? Who is *not* involved?
- What are the relationships between all those involved?
- Who is in charge? What is the status hierarchy?
- Who needs to know about this?
- Who needs to be influenced or persuaded?

Leadership: Questions about you as a role model

- How do I want to come across? How will I be and act as a change project leader?
- What kind of role model am I going to be?

Why? Questions about the motivation, commitment, rationale and values

A change project is important. Apart from costing a great deal of money, there have to be some human values driving it.

- Why do we need to change at all? What is the need we are meeting? Why now?
- What is at stake? What happens if we don't do this?
- Does it address something that matters? Is it emotionally engaging?
- Will people want to be part of it?
- How does this fit into the long-term plans of the organization?
- What's in it for us? For the company? For the shareholders?
- How will this benefit our society/humankind? (Think big!)

What and Where? Questions about the vision, mission and scope

- What resources do we need in terms of finance, skills, knowledge?
- What further opportunities would there be in the future?
- What else is likely to happen? What new set of challenges would arise?
- What are the limits or scope of this change?

- 🔖   How does this specific goal fit into the larger context?
- 🔖   How does this planned change mesh with the wider context – the current economic environment, current world events, and so on?
- 🔖   Does it open up further ideas and possibilities? Is it life-enhancing? (Does this vision come from the world of Abundance?)

How and When? Questions about the action, process, strategy and evidence

- 🔖   How are we actually going to achieve this?
- 🔖   What do we need to pay attention to?
- 🔖   What kinds of changes are we making?
- 🔖   How will we know when we have got what we want?
- 🔖   What kind of feedback will we get?
- 🔖   How easy will it be to change course if the situation changes?

IMPLEMENTATION

Test your imagined reality for coherence: Does it hang together logically? Does every proposed change lead somewhere useful? Are there any parts of the process which are *hopes* or *wishes* rather than firm commitments or considerations? A vision has to be more than just 'a good idea'. Some decisions are made to meet a need, but have not been thought through in terms of practicability. For example, the UK government was quick to adopt European policy on recycling old refrigerators to reduce the amount of CFCs being released into the atmosphere, but failed to set up adequate facilities for doing the actual work of dismantling them.

EVERY CHANGE HAS CONSEQUENCES

Explore some ' what if . . . ?' questions about the consequences of your actions, see yourself in that probable future, and notice what is different. Put yourself in the shoes of someone who has been on the receiving end of this change, and see it from their point of view. How has their life been changed? Here are some further questions to assist you in considering the impact of the changes you want to make.

Progress now

Gains and losses

If any of those of imagined changes or a specific change project that you are engaged in, were to become the next reality, consider:

- What would be the *gain* – personally, organizationally, nationally, globally?

- What would be the *loss* – personally, organizationally, nationally, globally?

Answering these questions is not simple. You may think that with really positive changes no one would lose anything important. But what often happens with major transformations is that as people learn new skills, gain new knowledge and understanding, their culture or way of thinking evolves, and they lose some of their previous expertise. For example, the educationist Kieran Egan (1997: 7) says 'when we become literate we do not cease to be oral-language users, but we do commonly lose some of the understanding that is a part of being exclusively an oral-language user.' Think about what your grandparents could do that you cannot, or that you have little understanding of as a result of changes in technology. For example, could you feed, clothe and transport yourself if current technology were to fail?

As cultures transform, people spread their talents more thinly. They have a wider range, but less intimate knowledge. This applies to their understanding of people as well as processes.

Progress now

Questions about the vision as a whole

If your vision, as it is now, were suddenly to manifest, what would be the downside? Put yourself in a King Midas frame of mind: what might you regret? An outside opinion on this could be extremely useful. Consider some probable outcomes:

- Does this vision give us hope for the future?
- Is it provocative, stimulating, challenging? To what extent does it open up further interesting ideas?
- What else would be easier to do if this were the case?
- Is it going to be fun to do this, rather than a boring chore . . .?

VISION STATEMENTS

To communicate your vision to others, you need to find a way of condensing all this information into something iconic: a vision statement, an image, emblem, symbol or metaphor, that will stimulate or even inspire other people. This requires much more than stringing a bunch of vaguely positive-sounding abstract nouns together to form a 'mission statement'. The challenge is to find a way of capturing the essence of the whole vision. A symbol or slogan that is designed to grab people's attention should be distinct, ear- and eye-catching. Think of how the title of a film or book grabs people's attention so that they want to know more about it, and are willing to invest their time and money in the experience. For example, Jeff Bezos, founder of online retailer Amazon, chose a company name that suggested the scale of what he would offer: every book in print. This vision worked: by 2002 Amazon was by far the largest internet bookseller in the UK.

Progress now

An icon of change . . .

Focus on the essence of the main message and find ways to represent your vision – in words, diagrams, cartoons, pictures, three-dimensional models, and so forth. Find an appropriate title, symbol or metaphor for your vision. Complete the sentences:

🖎 'My vision is like . . .'

🖎 'The title for this project is . . .'

Notice whatever comes to mind. Use this exercise to start the process; refine it later. At this stage you are gathering information. Each attempt at encapsulating the content of your vision is a closer approximation. Remember that 'good enough' is good enough! Find some appropriate symbols or representative objects, and then sort out your ideas by drawing them on paper or on a whiteboard, or by arranging them in the space around you. Once they are 'out there' they are much easier to arrange and structure. If they just stay in your mind they tend to remain a jumble of abstract concepts, fragments and hypotheses.

An icon, symbol or metaphor should:

- Be down-to-earth, sensible, have a point.
- Be understandable by all involved, and to those on the outside.
- Resonate with shared values.
- Inspire people to consider opportunities.

For example, Tim Smit refers to the Eden Project as *The Eighth Wonder of the World*, and *The United Nations of Plants* to communicate his vision. Although the 'Eighth Wonder of the World' is somewhat clichéd, it still has the power to motivate people.

SELLING THE VISION

Once clear about the vision, communicate it to everyone else involved. Look upon the next stage as your 'advertising campaign' which is designed to win the hearts and minds of everyone involved in the change project. The success of this project may depend on how well you do this. The term 'selling the vision' does not refer to commercial wheeling and dealing, but in the sense used to describe job interviews or presentations as selling yourself, selling your skills, selling your ideas – your uniqueness – to others.

One form of best practice is to tell a story. Storytelling is a major industry worldwide, covering news and media; book, film and TV production. Although storytelling may seem 'unconventional' in management terms, think about what inspirational speakers do. Management gurus travel the world, engaging audiences with stories of their achievements, company turnarounds, and so on. The intention is to inspire the audience so that they return to their workplaces sufficiently fired up to create their own great changes. Often it is these anecdotes of success that stay with people. Stories are excellent motivational devices, so use them to communicate your vision.

TELLING THE STORY

You will be more successful in bringing your vision to life for your audience when you are 'experiencing it from the inside' – as if you are actually there describing it enthusiastically as it unfolds, rather in the manner of an on-the-spot news-reporter. The richer it is for you, the more vivid it becomes for your audience. For example, make statements in the present continuous tense, the —ing forms: 'I am standing here watching the construction team bolt on the final strut that holds the whole building together . . .' It is your passion which has the greatest effect; anything half-hearted or lukewarm will not deliver. If you are not 100 per cent committed and enthusiastic about what you want to achieve, now is the time to quit this activity and go and do something else. No one will ever know about your dreams, because they wouldn't be sufficiently interested in hearing about them.

STORIES

The advantage of a story over an abstract business report is that the audience can imagine themselves to be in the world of the story. As the storyteller, you provide enough cues for them to construct their own imaginary version of your vision and then take them on a journey through it. For example, tell them to 'see the domes coming together like huge soap bubbles on the side of the quarry, as the yellow tower crane lifts each hexagon so that it can be bolted into place by the 'sky-monkeys' whom you can see up there silhouetted against the blue sky.' Any story that captures the audience's imagination generates an emotional response which will motivate them to action.

Generally speaking:

- Stories work best when you make them real for the audience by providing plenty of rich, sensory descriptions of where you are and what is happening.

- A story solves a problem, so state what the problem is early on.

- Stories are motivating when they engage the audience's emotions, values and desires. This is where your passion will rub off on them.

- People will relate to your vision only when they can see themselves as part of it. Put them *in* the vision so that they can experience it first-hand in their imaginations.

- Bring them back out again so that they can integrate that experience into their own lives.

- Indicate what the benefits are for them, why they should be involved. People will willingly engage in projects when they perceive an opportunity for using their talents, their skills and knowledge. Most people rise to a challenge.

- When people recognize that something is worthwhile, they will also acknowledge their own need for changing and learning.

- Make the boundaries explicit. A vision has limits: you are not going to change everything in the universe. So specify what will not be changing.

- Be genuine. Tell stories about yourself, your successes and failures, your own humanity.

- Refine the story by testing it on a trusted ally. Ask them to tell you what is unclear if they are getting confusing images in their mind.

Response to the story

Upon hearing the story, seeing the plans, envisaging 'everything changing,' people often experience fear of loss. This feeling of loss of the familiar may (temporarily) override the hope of gain. Generally speaking, people do not like surprises, especially when a significant part of their life is at stake. Be prepared for the feelings people will have about the change. They need to know:

- What exactly will be different?
- What will stay the same, and continue to function in more or less the same way?

And on a personal level:

- What will they gain?
- What will they lose?

People need time to assimilate information and work through the implications. Therefore it is a good idea to provide follow-up reference material – text, charts, diagrams, drawing – so that they can check the information at their own speed, and ask clarifying questions as necessary. If you only give a 'bare-bones' presentation of the facts: 'This is what we propose: X will go; Y will take its place. This will take Z amount of time', people often only hear the first piece of 'shocking news' about eliminating X, and start fantasizing worst-case scenarios. Or they go 'into denial' – which means they switch off and hear nothing else, and you will be wasting your time.

As people familiarize themselves with the vision, they feel more involved and begin to assume ownership of it: 'This is my role; this is how I can contribute; this is how I fit in.' The more they see the overall values and benefits for everyone concerned, including the customers, the more the project team becomes aligned and committed to the vision.

Eventually people will start on the actual change work – but not yet. All this thinking about the project needs to happen first. You want to avoid possible pitfalls, objections and resistance, so the more thought you put into this now, the easier it will be later when you come to physically do it.

IF STORYTELLING REALLY ISN'T YOUR THING . . .

Adapt the following outline to meet your needs.

- ◊ State the facts, rather than spout propaganda. Most people are well able to recognize 'political posturing'.

- ◊ Sell the benefits of the change. Assure people that this is not just change for change's sake.

- ◊ Although people may groan when another change looms, they will come on board if you give them the information in the 'right' way for them. Therefore get to know their preferences, or generally cover a number of learning styles (see Chapter 6). For example: If they prefer everything at once, send them to an exhibition or display of the project, with books, diagrams, models, and so on. Others only need to know about what affects them directly. Anything more, they switch off.

- ◊ Explain the future work patterns, and how you will improve lines of communication. As change leader you need to be open with everyone, ready to listen to people, anywhere, any time, so that you know what is going on, and ensure that everything important gets passed on to the rest of the team. It is essential to keep staff and other managers informed about progress: don't leave them in the dark needlessly. Answer all questions honestly, without prevarication.

SPREADING THE WORD

Once the project is under way, and changes are beginning to show in the outside world, the press, the competition, the general public are probably going to react to what is happening. Those people only have partial knowledge of the details, or have had second- or third-hand reports from those with a limited view or a definite bias. So consider and plan:

- How you will handle this wider dissemination during the various stages of the project.
- What you can do to ensure that they get the right impression or message.
- How to address the issues: 'What's in it for us? How will the world be a better place as a result?'

GETTING IT DONE – PROJECT MANAGEMENT

A change project needs to be well planned (which is where project management comes in) before it is implemented. Tasks must be allocated so that people know their role in the project. If everyone knows their skills and talents are being used to the full, and that every job is important, they are more likely to add their own particular value to the scheme.

As the project progresses, check how things are working out in reality. There will be unforeseen snags and benefits, so you need to closely monitor the feedback you are getting. What plans do you have in place for dealing with significant deviations from the plans? Do you have a system for adjusting your course when your star moves across the sky?

ENJOYMENT

Make it easy for everyone to enjoy what they are doing. A vision worth striving for will produce challenges, hardships and enjoyment as it begins to materialize. Ask people directly: 'What would be fun for you?' When people are doing what they enjoy, they engage with life more fully, and work with other people in a spirit of cooperation. You will be delighted by their display of talent and creativity as you bounce ideas back and forth.

As the project develops, everyone will be able to see how it is progressing, where it leads to, the contingencies, opportunities and possibilities for revision. Some of the ideas that arise you run with; others are put away for possible future use.

In the next chapter you will be revisiting your own resource bank, remembering your skills and talents, and identifying the source of your own fun in life.

CHAPTER 4
Self-awareness

If the doors of perception were cleansed
everything would appear to Man as it is:
infinite. For Man has closed himself up, till he
sees all things through narrow chinks of his
cavern.

WILLIAM BLAKE,
THE MARRIAGE OF HEAVEN AND HELL

No one can develop anyone else apart from
himself. The door to development is locked
from the inside.

CHRIS ARGYRIS

STARTING IN THE FAMILIAR WORLD

How well do you know yourself? What do you personally have to offer the change project in terms of your skills, abilities, knowledge and resources? Your weaknesses may be only too obvious, but what are your strengths, your life-enhancing attitudes, preferences and beliefs? This chapter provides an opportunity for you to get to know yourself in detail, by finding out what you bring to a change project. It is vital to be aware of your beliefs about change and learning, as they affect what happens, and influence your ability to respond appropriately to others.

Because you seem so familiar to yourself, it is easy to take your talents for granted and think of your abilities as 'ordinary'. So how would it be if instead you see yourself as sitting on a gold mine of personal wisdom? Maybe now is the time to assess your riches, to unearth these buried nuggets and bring them into the daylight. There is always more to be learned from your experiences. Although they are part of your 'history', when you pay attention to them again they become renewed in the light of what you now know. Hindsight offers great opportunities for finding new meanings and greater understanding of the events in your life.

Progress now

Attitude to change

Attitudes towards change vary considerably. Do you:

- 🔃 Live in a world where 'the only constant is change'?
- 🔃 Welcome change? Do you seek out opportunities for change? 'Time to learn something new!'
- 🔃 Only change when you are forced to, or resist it as much as possible? 'No more! I've had enough change for a while!'
- 🔃 Anticipate deviations from your plans, and allow for contingencies?

How do other members of the project team figure in this? Are you all similar, or do you go to extremes? If anyone resists certain kinds of change, what do you need to do about that?

RESOURCES

Memories of past successes are a wonderful resource for being in a good state now. Thinking analytically about those events means that you can also learn more from them. Although some memories come unbidden at odd moments, you can have more control over them if you sit quietly and specify which memories you want to recall. Be explicit. Stipulate, 'a time when I was doing X' or 'when I was feeling Y'. Holding that focus in your mind, allow your mind to come up with the relevant memories. Trust the process; you will get answers when you ask questions or make requests. Think of the mind as a friendly librarian, who brings you only as much as you can deal with. You do not need everything at once!

Progress now
Remember a time when . . .

Looking back, you label some of the significant changes you made as 'hard' or 'easy'. Decide what these terms mean to you. If you are requesting others to carry out similar searches, let them evaluate their memories in their own way.

🕊 Think of a change that was *hard* to make. See the events in your mind's eye, and note what transpired.

🕊 Now think of a change that was *easy* to make. Again, watch what happens in that memory.

Your task is to identify the key pieces that make change hard or easy. What are the critical factors? Do you attribute the results to causes outside your control (such as environmental influences or 'fate'), or can you take responsibility for them? One way of teasing these factors out is to compare and contrast two similar events and notice what appears to be making the difference.

With two experiences in mind, mentally step back so that you can see them both.

🕊 What were the differences between a *hard* change and an *easy* change?

🕊 What are the key factors?

Check out your hypothesis with some further examples to test the validity of the likely factors.

Progress now

Reasons for change

Here are some statements about reasons for change. Decide which is closest to the way you think about change. Then decide which is the furthest from the way you think.

◊ Change because it is needed: 'There has to be a better way', 'How could this be better?', 'It is always possible to improve the system.'

◊ Change for change's sake: 'The system/process has been here for X years, and it's time to change', 'Anything over five years old is obsolete and must be replaced', 'It's past its sell-by date', 'Change is always implemented at New Year.'

◊ Change for others: 'I want other people to be more efficient, effective in what they do.'

◊ Change for self: 'I want to make this work for me/make my life easier', 'How can I improve this?', 'It is personally satisfying to find better ways of doing things.'

If you think your way of doing things is (or ought to be) universal, remember that other people think differently. Should you forget, your mis-communications and misunderstandings will remind you.

EAGERNESS FOR CHANGE

How would you rate your eagerness for change? Here are five descriptive categories applied to the stage at which people engage with a change or innovation.

1. **Pioneers** are out there in front, with the latest gadgets, starting trends that others follow. They want whatever is new. To be a pioneer company means spending budget on research and development with no surety that the investment will be rewarded. But you are first in the field. Look, for example, at those who rushed into the market for third-generation mobile phones. The professors of marketing, Jagdish Sheth and Rajendra Sisodia (2002), point out that:

    The truth is, companies that are No. 1 in their industry are usually the least innovative, although they may have the largest R&D budget. . . . The typical sequence in most industries is that No. 3 innovates, No. 1 copies (and therefore validates), and No. 2 follows. This holds true for both product and process innovation. No. 1 companies should adopt a fast-follower strategic posture when it comes to innovation. It seems radical and counterintuitive, but for No. 1 firms, the risks of innovating outweigh most of the benefits the innovation brings.

2. Next to arrive are the **Joiners**, willing to jump on the bandwagon as soon as they know it is safe, that the bugs have been removed. Their slogan is: 'Me Too!' Being second has advantages: you can learn from the mistakes that have already been made, and build better and cheaper. However, this does not threaten the pioneers because they have already moved on to the next innovation. For example, rivals to Dyson's vortex vacuum cleaner are on the market at a cheaper price. Dyson moved on to washing machines.

3. With refined technology and mass-produced components, the market follows the recipe and sells 'standard' models. The **Early Majority** sees the trend and adopts what they perceive as the fashion. They often benefit from cheaper, more reliable products, though with 'bells and whistles' that they will never use. For example, how many of the features on your video recorder do you use or even understand?

4. By the time the **Late Majority** get involved, there are already counterfeit imitations of what will soon be going out of fashion. With management fads, the original message has been transmuted into a watered-down, Chinese-whispered version that has lost its spirit.

5. Finally, the **Laggards** resist until the last moment, reluctantly admitting: 'I suppose I have to . . .'. It could be a forced

technological change that finally gets them, as with the proposed change from analogue to digital television. Commercially they could be creating niche markets in antiques or anything using 'traditional values'. For example, mid-twentieth-century valve-based radios are now collectable. Another approach is to use traditional technology – wrought-iron work, stone masonry – to create personalized products.

This cycle demonstrates a shift from thinking about an idea, to the product that meets a need, to the technology of producing it, to the benefits that it offers and the values it supports. Finally, someone will see a missed opportunity with an old technology, and start on a new tack.

RATE OF CHANGE

People cope admirably when change happens at the rate they are comfortable with. However, it is a common belief that the rate of change is increasing. Being dragged through life provides scant time for drawing breath as you try to keep up with events. It is as if you are in the thrall of external powers, and feel stressed, and no longer in control of your own life. When life moves at a slower pace, you have time to notice what is going on – or you get bored because you are not getting sufficient stimulation. There will certainly be times when life does not match your preference, and you will feel some kind of discomfort.

You may entertain the notion that there is a 'proper' speed at which change occurs; when events unfold at your preferred rate, you feel more in control. As with all individual preferences, you need to be aware of other people's preferences, because it is highly probable that they will like events to unfold at a different rate. Being significantly out of sync could create problems around rate of work, deadlines, and so on. This links with notions of time (see Chapter 5).

SKILLS AND RESOURCES

Knowing where you are going is one thing; the resources you have available will determine whether or not you get there. Therefore it is important to identify what you are already good at: your skills, abilities, motivations, interests – in fact, everything that could be useful. You may have thought about your transferable skills when filling in a job application or performance review. But maybe you missed some . . .

Skills get taken for granted, part of who you are. You may then downgrade your competence, seeing your unique skills as 'ordinary', even 'trivial.' You might assume that others have those same abilities until you discover them floundering, or telling you, 'I wish I could do that as well as you can.' The answer to 'Doesn't everybody do that?' is 'No they don't!'

Progress now

'Trivial' things you are good at

Make a list of your skills which you consider 'ordinary' or 'trivial':

- What do you do that you are good at, but which seems ordinary or trivial? If you are uncertain, ask people who know you well.

- What do you perform at the level of 'unconscious competence'? That is, what skill can you demonstrate without thinking about it?

For example, trivial skills might be: sorting things out, keeping things tidy, telling jokes or stories, judging distance or the weight and size of things, organizing social events, improvising, listening to other people, designing with style, meeting people and making them feel comfortable, finding your way around in unfamiliar places, finding bargains, getting good value, getting people to see things from different points of view, multitasking – doing several activities at once.

Examine your list of skills, and decide how each of them could be useful in the process of implementing change.

Because the future is unknowable, having useful transferable skills is going to assist your understanding of the new order of things. Think back to when you arrived in a new place, a new organization, and you had to 'find your feet' and 'learn your way around'. What strategies have you already devised for joining new teams, groups or organizations?

RETAINING THE ESSENTIALS

> Once you have crossed the river, there is no need to carry the boat on your back.
>
> Chinese proverb

Change does not necessarily mean eliminating all traces of the past. Being a 'new broom' and sweeping away everything could mean you lose valuable resources, things that already work well. People want to feel special, and may want to hang on to their particular expertise, regardless of how obsolete it has become. For example, being an expert in 1980s software packages may be admirable, but not immediately useful. However, rather than simply abandoning those skills, it would be more valuable to transfer the skills gained in acquiring that expertise, and find ways of applying the general principles in new contexts. In times of change you need a reliable bank of resources, and the ability to adapt and improvise. Similarly, keeping knowledge to yourself, in order to retain power, is becoming increasingly difficult, given the ease at which information is passed around the internet. Specific sensitive information often has a short shelf-life; it rapidly moves into the public domain, or it becomes obsolete.

SIGNALS FOR CHANGE

> To act with foresight, the company must act on signals, rather than on pain.
>
> DE GEUS, 1997: 40

The warning bells ring; the water is rising fast! A crisis demands your attention. What do you do? Leap into action? Wait awhile in case it's a false alarm? Hanging back could lead to crisis management: the more you delay, the less time there will be for planning the best course of action. With only one perceived option you feel compelled to take it to stop things getting worse (you hope), and end up 'fire-fighting' instead of dealing with the real issue. Denial, as a strategy, is a limiting human trait. So how long will you ignore the wake up signal? Or to put it another way: How bad does it have to get before you take action?

If you had time, you might stop and wonder: 'Why is this crisis in my life now? Did I not notice the warning signs? If so, what were the indicators that things were changing? What stopped me from seeing them? What stopped me from acting?'

KNOWING IT IS TIME TO CHANGE

Build it and he will come.

FIELD OF DREAMS, 1989

The time to consider your options is before a crisis arrives. What should you be paying attention to? How do you select from all the signals arriving from the world around us, and from within? Some will be extremely relevant to your continuing existence, both individually and organizationally. You have to decide which to act on, which to keep an eye on, and which to ignore. Therefore you need to identify the key indicators that tell you: 'Pay attention!'

Progress now

Response style

What is your usual way of responding to a wake-up call?

1 Act immediately

Assume the information is valid and relevant, that something has to be done.

This could mean checking sources, ensuring the facts are as they first appear, and preparing to take further action if necessary. Action stops when there is evidence to the contrary.

2 Do nothing

Assume it is a false alarm, or 'scare story' which will blow over in time.

🔃 If you have a policy of 'wait and see' before doing anything, how long do you wait? If now is 'too early', how long will it be before it is 'too late'?

🔃 You wait until other people tell you – or rise up in rebellion!

3 Set thresholds

In between these two extremes there are many variations:

🔃 The amount of evidence has to reach a certain threshold before positive action is taken.

🔃 Time has to pass before any action is taken. You wait to see what happens, ascertain whether it is an anomaly, a 'flash in the pan', or a sustained change.

4 Act when a threshold is reached

🐚 How much evidence do you need?

🐚 Which source of evidence is most potent?

   🐚 From within – based on your own experience and intuitions?

   🐚 From others – based on your trust relationship over time?

🐚 How many times must it happen?

🐚 How many independent sources have to provide corroborating information?

5 Act after a period of time

🐚 How long do you wait? Is there a set time – days, weeks, months – or does it depend on other factors, such as impact assessment?

🐚 What do you do during this time? Do you just wait it out, or are you engaged in researching the evidence or watching key indicators?

6 Act constantly

You proactively seek information on anything that might affect your business.

Progress now

Time lag

Recall an event where, when you look back, you think you could have taken action sooner. Only later did you realize you had missed the clues, or had had other things on your mind which prevented you from taking appropriate action.

🕭 How long was it from the time you first noticed the signs of change until decisive action was taken?

🕭 How many times did you need to be exposed to the evidence before realizing it was significant?

Is that typical of you? Think of some further examples in the same way, and begin to notice if there is a pattern in your response.

EXTERNAL EVENTS

'Look around. Pay attention to what is happening.' Easy to say, but what exactly are you looking for? If you are tracking deviations from the norm, this presupposes you know what the norm is. Statistical information can be gathered on processes that repeat over time. But every process has random fluctuations as a matter of course, and you need to decide: is this particular deviation within the range, or is it something exceptional? If you are introducing a new process, such a decision will be hard to make as there are as yet no baseline measurements of what is 'normal'.

Progress now
What kind of evidence has the most potency for you?

What do you pay attention to? Identify some of the indicators for your own particular business. For example, historical trends, technology changes, world events.

In the business world, trends, cycles and growth patterns can be observed. Information technology advances; thinking changes – eventually!

Progress now

Changing your mind

During a change project your original ideas will usually need to be modified. There will be times whey you deliberately deviate from your earlier plans. Recall a time when you changed your mind about something quite important. Identify the critical factors, major influences, events, that made it important for you to change.

Was it someone else . . .

- Telling you that you were wrong?
- Arguing logically for an alternative?
- Getting you to evaluate your decision in a different context?
- Humiliating you by pointing out your inadequacies, your faults?
- Suggesting: 'Think about it in this way . . .'?

Or did you . . .

- 🍃 Re-evaluate the evidence of your own experience: 'I can do this!'?
- 🍃 Think it through, holding the belief: 'There has to be a better way'?
- 🍃 Go back to first principles: 'What is really going on here? How does this really work?'
- 🍃 Wonder: 'How else could I do this?'
- 🍃 Consider the consequences: 'If I were to do X, then Y or even Z could happen'?

TO CHANGE OR NOT TO CHANGE

People resist change out of habit. The stronger a habit, the more it takes to change it. 'If it works, why do anything different?' 'If it ain't broke . . . ' However, people experience pulls in two directions. They seek consistency and predictability, and develop habits in the way they shop, eat, entertain themselves, and so on. They also seek novelty, variety, and avoid boredom by creating diversions from routine. However, they may only make small excursions into the unknown, while clinging to what they know. In that way, there is a get-out if it exceeds their comfort threshold.

Every innovation has its associated risks, and people tend to be risk averse. Because of the unpredictability of change, even when the intentions are good, there is still the risk that you will not get the results you want; that the technology will not work properly; or there will be unforeseen side effects or consequences. People will change habitual behaviour only when something significantly better is on offer, and they can imagine the benefits. If the perceived risks outweigh the expected benefits, nothing happens. When they understand the risks but consider them unimportant, or that they will be able to cope with them should they arise, they will go ahead.

Resistance

You probably know where your own particular resistance to change lies. Resistance means not wanting to experience certain states or take specific actions because they are associated with negative feelings or memories. Common reasons for inaction are fear:

- of the unknown (you do not want to lose control).
- of 'not knowing' (you will appear stupid – asking questions lowers your status).
- of hurting others (you mind-read what others are thinking and feeling, without checking).
- of being wrong, of making mistakes (you forget that this is how you learn).
- of confusion (you forget that understanding comes as you restructure information).

You have a choice: plunge in and do something different; or hold on to your limitations and hope the fear or pain will go away. Whatever you decide, you need to assess the consequences. Maybe it is time to examine the validity of the fear. Self-preservation and personal integrity are worthy reasons; avoiding something imaginary needs to be investigated. You do not have to confront your fears head on. Despite what some therapists suggest, 'reliving' your fears does not necessarily lead to being in a more resourceful state. Fighting a fear by simply going against it does not respect your personal ecology. How about simply changing your mind about those fears, or just getting bored with having them?

HEALTHY FEARS

Some fears are justified. It is sensible to refuse to do anything that is life-threatening, or violates your values. You probably want to avoid deals that are 'too good to be true', 'easy money', and 'get rich quick' schemes. Suspect any 'with one bound he was free' solutions that gloss over serious difficulties. 'We'll take care of that. Don't worry about it' should arouse intense curiosity.

Lack of knowledge

If you do not see the big picture yet, you may just need to be patient for things to unfold. If you lack information then you know what to find out. If other people are uncertain or confused, help them to clarify their position.

Lack of confidence

You may lack confidence because you have simply not rehearsed an activity sufficiently. Find safe ways of practising those skills so that they become second nature, or no big deal. There are plenty of books and courses on confidence building. The hardest part may be acknowledging that you have a gap in your learning, because you think it lowers your status in the eyes of others.

Lack of social awareness

If you are concerned about fitting into an established group who are relatively unknown to you, find a trusted confidant who will explain the culture of the group and tell you 'how we do things around here'. Groups are generally forgiving at first, so take advice, and learn fast. If you are uncertain how others perceive your position and status in the group, then model yourself on the most confident high-status leaders you know. The project team will accord you high status so long as your official position is matched by your personal integrity and authenticity.

Lack of enthusiasm

There are just some things you don't get excited about. If certain aspects of the project – accountancy, project management, negotiation, or fund-raising – leave you cold, then you had better delegate this function to someone else. But you still need to know the basics in order to oversee the change project.

Your lack of enthusiasm could be the result of a lack of understanding – you do not yet see how all the pieces fit together. If you want to know why something is important, find an

enthusiastic expert with a passion for this particular topic (and with good rapport skills), and have them explain it to you. You could also imagine being that person and seeing things through their eyes. Could you congruently argue the case from their point of view? You do not have to become a fanatic. Seeing from their point of view will broaden your awareness and sensitivity.

ACCEPTANCE

Self-awareness means knowing what you have by way of skills and resources, recognizing your biases and preferences. As you acknowledge your own uniqueness, you get a sense of how other people are different from you. People perceive the world in very different ways, in terms of what matters to them, the rules they live and work by, their interests and enthusiasms. If you want to communicate to them in a way they will understand, you need to move towards matching their way of understanding.

Resistance, blocks and fears come and go, often without doing very much at all. Sometimes you may have no idea of what you did that worked. However, the way you encode your experience in words often hinders change. We turn to this linguistic analysis of the metaphors we use in the next chapter.

CHAPTER 5

Metaphors of Change

A word fitly spoken is like apples of gold in pictures of silver.

PROVERBS 25: 11

There is no means of distinguishing the supposedly real thing from the metaphorical thing. What we take to be the real thing is merely the most common way the thing is seen, or described.

LAWSON, 2001: 17–18

METAPHORS

Metaphors are far more common than you might suppose. Although they are usually thought of as 'poetic' or as a fantasy part of language, in fact, *all* language is metaphorical because it *transfers* meaning from what you already know to what is unfamiliar. Finding some aspect that two experiences have in common allows you to make a meaningful connection between them. You begin to comprehend the new experience by transferring across the relevant parts of your existing knowledge.

For example, the people who named new computer technology chose metaphors based on:

- **Form**. The pointing device is called a *mouse* because it is shaped vaguely like the rodent, and has a connecting cable that looks like a tail.

- **Function**. We *open* windows containing icons which resemble miniature manilla folders; we *save* documents which resemble sheets of paper. A computer provides the illusion that we are engaging in the familiar activities of typing words or drawing pictures on paper.

We use metaphors such as *vision* or *mission* for things that we want, and *blocks* or *barriers* for what stops us getting them. Ultimately these limit our understanding. The metaphors are useful in certain contexts, but their associations may restrict our thinking when we need alternatives. For example, if you think of a barrier, what comes to mind? Perhaps the image of a fence, or a wall? Is there a way round or through? If your thinking is in a rut, or your ideas are being channelled in one direction, you may need to plough some new furrows in order to change. A 'line in the sand' may be more easily – or inadvertently – crossed. By thinking of something stopping you as a challenge, different associations apply. Any metaphor can help or hinder you; changing the metaphors in use may be much simpler and more fun than other kinds of change. The point about metaphors is not that they make communication more entertaining, but that the language you use affects how you think and what you do. Therefore it is important to notice which metaphors are in use, because you can then influence how people think.

Progress now

Metaphorical relationships

Start thinking metaphorically by coming up with metaphors to describe some of your relationships. Complete the statement: 'My relationship with X is like . . .'.

For example, you might come up with metaphors such as:

- ❧ Climbing a mountain.
- ❧ Walking on eggshells.
- ❧ Going round and round in a revolving door.

And then find the connections with: 'Because . . .'

- ❧ . . . we are roped together.
- ❧ . . . it could collapse at any moment.
- ❧ . . . there is no way out.

Progress now

Myself as change manager

Now think about how you would like to be seen as a change manager. Complete the statement: 'As a change manager I want to be like . . .'. The possibilities are limitless! You might, for example, choose metaphors such as:

- A gardener, nurturing tender plants.
- The ringmaster in a circus.
- A pilot boat guiding ocean liners into harbour.

Another way to approach this is to draw a picture, cartoon or diagram of how you see yourself working on a change project. This does not have to be realistic. For example, you might draw an open door, a sponge, a Sherlock Holmes figure, a mountaineer, and so on.

METAPHORS FOR THE CHANGE PROCESS

In the 'change is a journey' metaphor, a change manager becomes a leader or explorer with a mission who leaves the well-trodden ways and treks into uncharted territory. Change means crossing a threshold into an unknown world. However, this limits your thinking if you only consider journeys. Other metaphors alter how you perceive change. For example, you may do things very differently if you see change as the unfolding of a flower, or the way a garden evolves. Other change metaphors provide different understanding:

- Fermentation – as in baking bread, brewing beer, creating a vintage.
- Evolution – as in the life cycle of plants, or the development of species of creatures.
- Attrition – the effect of wind and rain on stone or the landscape.
- Randomness – shuffling cards, rolling dice, or picking up pebbles from a beach.

Adapt a metaphor to improve the fit with experience. The power of metaphor is the extent to which it allows you to make new connections and see what was previously hidden.

ORGANIZATIONAL METAPHORS

People at the top of organizations often express their attitude and aspirations using symbolic metaphors. For instance, some CEOs (chief executive officers) see business as a form of warfare, which implies that their competitors are 'the enemy'. While out in the field, reconnoitring the territory, it may be wise to watch out for the big guns, keep your head down and avoid the flak. Organizations and teams often use such symbolism to define how they work, and to indicate how individuals and competitors are perceived. For example, if you perceive other businesses as enemies, it may help to create some 'fighting spirit' which bonds members of the group together, so that they will do better. On the other hand, it could make it hard to see them as cooperative friends – which would be desirable for sharing expertise.

The implications of the dominant metaphor may inhibit innovation. The 'business is war' model leads to *winners* and *losers*. If you lose, you are out of the game. If people adopt the attitude of 'all's fair in love and war', then it could be very difficult to get people to consider anyone else's point of view or values, or introduce changes designed to enhance personal integrity, congruence, collaboration, or even explore spiritual values. According to organizational consultant, Robert J. Marshak, 'Members of the organization just "won't get it".' The typical response might be something like: 'What does that have to do with business?' Unless or until the metaphorical field is modified to include or accentuate a different core theme(s), the organization's reality and response will be driven out by a 'wartime mentality'. (Marshak, 1996: 152–3.)

The metaphors a company use indicate the kind of culture you are dealing with. This means you could get rapport with them by using similar language; or you may decide you do not want to be around people who think like that!

You need to know which metaphors will unite and inspire the project team. The following metaphor exercises should soon have people bouncing ideas off each other. Each person states their metaphor and the presuppositions they are aware of. Other members of the group give their responses and any associations. Sharing metaphors brings up ideas that you may not have thought of, but which you recognize as appropriate or stimulating. Laughter is a good test of relevance! Remember that these exercises are not deeply analytical; nor are there 'right' answers. Inventing metaphors is a process of successive approximation. Lateral thinking is intuitive, and needs a good sense of humour! Go with whatever bubbles to the surface and see where it takes you. People bond as they share their ideas; everyone learns about the group and each other.

Progress now

What would be a good metaphor for your team, group, company or organization? Create a statement which applies to your professional, business or work context. It would be useful to do this in a group. Complete the sentence with a metaphor or simile: 'My organization is like . . .'.

For example, you may think of it in terms of machinery, a means of transport, a living organism, or be reminded of some scene involving characters in a story or movie:

🔾 'We're on a bus, and several people are fighting to get into the driver's seat.'

🔾 'It's as if we are on a cruise ship with a busy schedule of ports to visit.'

🔾 'It's like living on *Big Brother*; they watch every move you make.'

LIFE'S A CIRCUS

How does a group or team perceive itself? Choose a metaphor such as a circus, which involves several people engaged in a defined set of tasks. How would you allocate the different roles among your group? What role would *you* have? You may see yourself as the ringmaster, but what if you were a lion-tamer, or bare-back rider? Who are the clowns in the group? Who trains animals, who is in charge of advance publicity or ticket sales? Who erects the tent; who walks the high-wire?

Progress now
Evaluating the metaphor

When you have explored your metaphor in detail, decide to what extent this is metaphor useful. If it is useful, then:

🔃 What are the positive consequences of living with this metaphor? (Remember, this does not have to be for all time. Use a metaphor only for as long as it offers something useful.)

🔃 What are its limitations?

If it does not fit, what metaphor would work better?

METAPHORS FOR TIME

Time like an ever rolling stream
Bears all its sons away

ISAAC WATTS: HYMN,
'O GOD OUR HELP IN AGES PAST'

Change happens over time. An unremarkable statement, perhaps, but consider what it tells us about how we conceive of time. Time is an abstraction: we know time has 'passed' because things are different somehow. For things that stay the same, time 'stands still'.

By joining *past* and *future* we create a *time-line*. Linear time suggests a path, journey or development. It presupposes that time has a continuous movement which only goes one way; once things have happened they are gone for ever. We use the time-line metaphor to depict historical events sequentially. The expressions: 'putting the past behind us' and 'looking forward to the future', suggest a time-line running from behind us to in front. For project management and planning, you need to observe the whole time line at one moment, in order to work with it logically and efficiently. In this 'year-planner mode' the past is usually way over to the left and the future off to the right (which matches the Western habit of writing from left to right).

Progress now

Finding time

Think about your relationship to time:

- 🕸 Do you move through time as if you were crossing a landscape?
- 🕸 Or are you stationary with time 'flowing' past you in the manner of Isaac Watts' stream?

Time metaphors are often spatial. Where do your locate time in space? Using one arm, point to the past. Use the other arm to point to the future. Are you pointing back and front, or to each side, or somewhere else? How do other people do this? Do they do it differently?

Progress now

Different experiences of time

We conceive of time in different ways, depending upon what we are doing. For example, time may drag or rush past, or we may be unaware of it.

What is your experience of time when you are:

- Busily engaged in an important task?
- Planning and monitoring a project?
- Socializing with your friends?
- Musing on the ideas presented to you in this book?

Perhaps you feel 'out of time', or 'going with the flow'. Do you become so engaged that you lose track of time or are unaware of time passing? When you are actively engaged in work, or playing sport, *now* is what matters.

METAPHORS OF LIMITATION

> All our truths are, in a sense, fictions – they are stories we choose to believe.

LAWSON, 1989, P. XXVIII

There are clues to how people limit themselves in the metaphors they use to describe their problems and difficulties. Language is often both the cause of the difficulty and the leverage point for intervening in order to get problems moving again. All it takes is a little imagination.

Earlier you were thinking about the *barrier* metaphor. Although people have their own associations for this, generally a barrier:

- Separates two areas.
- Is something fairly solid or substantial.
- Stands between you and where you want to go; or it prevents other things or people getting into where you are.

Progress now

Barriers

Are there any barriers that confront you in your proposed change project? If so, explore in your mind's eye:

🐍 For whom is this a barrier?

🐍 What kind of barrier is it? What is it made of? How big is it?

🐍 What does it stop people doing, or where does it stop them going?

Maybe these restraints are just figments of your imagination. It is your mind that is stopping you moving to a more desirable place. What happens when you envision: 'It's not a barrier, . . .

🐍 . . . it's just a gate'?

🐍 . . . it's just a line painted on the ground'?

🐍 . . . it's a door which I can open with a key'?

You can think of other variations. Each metaphor implies different ways of traversing some kind of threshold. If the only thing stopping you from taking a step forward is the language you are using, that tells you the best place to begin work.

METAPHORS FOR PROBLEMS

Here are some common metaphors for problems:

Table 5.1 Metaphors for problems

No movement	Stuck, fixed, blocked, no room to move, caught up, lost the key.
Obstructed	Barrier, bottleneck, obstacle course.
Mechanical failure	Impotent, broken, weak, spanner in the works, choked.
Uncreative	Dried up, bored, sterile, uninspired.
Conflicted	Embattled, at war, digging in, entrenched, refusing to cross enemy lines.
Lack of clarity	Confused, in a fog, obscured, scrambled, lost sight of.
Indecisive	At a crossroads, at sixes and sevens, between a rock and a hard place.

COMMUNICATING IN METAPHORS

Communication works best when you have some idea of how other people perceive the world. You will get clues from the metaphors they use to describe their difficulties and limitations. You know their current metaphor is not working, so anything that changes or extends it is worth trying. As a change manager you can notice which metaphor seems to be in use and then ask people to begin to explore their own options as in the previous exercise.

Unsticking stuckness

Hamlet: Denmark's a prison.

Rosencrantz: Then is the world one.

Hamlet: A goodly one; in which there are many confines, wards and dungeons, Denmark being one o' the worst.

Rosencrantz: We think not so, my lord.

Hamlet: Why, then, 'tis none to you; for there is nothing either good or bad, but thinking makes it so: to me it is a prison.

HAMLET, ACT II: 2

Language is a prison when it defines or 'fixes' the world. Stuckness arises out of a belief that 'this is the way it is'. A strongly held truth allows for no possible movement, no way out, no possible path. People get boxed in, unable to envisage any legitimate moves or actions because of the imposed constraints: 'It's against the rules. I'm not allowed to do X.'

You may find out where the rules come from, by inquiring: 'Who says you can/can't do this?' If the other person is uncertain of the guiding principles, suggest they make up a rule: 'If there were a rule here, what would it be?', 'What guidelines or principles would fit your beliefs?' Truths usually change over time, so find out when the stuckness occurred: 'Has this always been the case?'

Change the way you perceive an issue by letting go of metaphorical limitations such as barriers and prisons, and choose instead metaphors that allow more openness and expand choices. For instance, instead of seeing the glass of water as half full or half empty, see it as containing the essence of life, or as a symbolic offering from the well of wisdom. Instead of having a 'problem', see it as an 'opportunity' or 'challenge' or even a message that it is time to think differently. If someone claims to be stuck, suggest they 'stand back' – literally or metaphorically – and notice exactly how they are 'sticking themselves'. When they know their limiting strategy, help them find a new metaphor that will work for them. Reframing is the art of changing your mind. Each shift of position – literal and metaphorical – creates an alternative point of view, throws new light on the issue, and opens up the realms of possibility.

People use different images to motivate themselves. It may take a while to fire some people up, and they need a head of steam before they roll into action. Others are firing on all cylinders and just need the starting signal. With some people, once they get the bit between their teeth, they are away, and you may need to have them on a short rein if they are too excited. When it comes to metaphors, it's horses for courses.

METAPHORS FOR VISIONS

In Chapter 3 you found a metaphor or symbol that captured the essence of your vision. The metaphor should relate closely to the goal or purpose you have in mind.

Progress now

The art gallery metaphor

Allow your mind to find some ideas that symbolize your vision:

Imagine you are visiting a gallery showing pictures of possible futures and desirable outcomes. Look around and let your eye alight on any picture that appeals to you. The great thing about this gallery is that you can have anything you want. You can combine parts of one picture with those of another to create the perfect image.

This art gallery will always be there when you need it. You could even have it as a multi-screen cinema with several movies playing simultaneously. Enter whenever you like, stay just as long as it remains interesting, and take away from this experience what you need to inspire your thinking.

CHANGING METAPHORS

When you get stuck in your thinking, change your point of view, literally or metaphorically. Changing your metaphors is an easy way to develop mental flexibility. The *change is a journey* metaphor involves moving to an alternative reality mode by crossing a threshold, such as when Dorothy in *The Wizard of Oz* is transported from Kansas to the Land of Oz. The *change is unfolding* metaphor implies there is nowhere to go. You are already there. You have what you need. All you have to do is nurture your existing talents and abilities, and allow your wisdom to bear fruit. This will yield a fine harvest!

Progress now

Learning metaphors

Chapter 6 continues the unfolding metaphor as you investigate your preferred way of learning. What would be a good metaphor for learning? Learning is like . . . ? What do these metaphors suggest to you about learning?

- ♫ Loading a new piece of software into your computer.
- ♫ Dropping a stone into a pond, and watching the ripples spread out.
- ♫ Planting a seed and letting it grow.

CHAPTER 6
Learning

O this learning, what a thing it is!
GREMIO IN *THE TAMING OF THE SHREW*, ACT I:1

Ask people . . . to recall two or three of the most important learning experiences in their lives and they will . . . tell you . . . of times when continuity ran out on them, when they had no past experience to fall back on, no rules or handbook. They survived, however, and came to count it as learning, as a growth experience.

CHARLES HANDY

HORSE SENSE

In recent years, thanks to the work of Monty Roberts (Roberts, 2000), we have learned how it is possible to communicate to horses using their own equine 'body-language'. The traditional way of 'breaking' a horse is based on fear and punishment; it is inefficient and becoming inappropriate or 'unacceptable'. Roberts uses the positive metaphor 'Join-Up' – the horse *chooses* to be with the human being, and is willing to let the trainer be the leader.

The Join-Up process is now included in some management training courses. Although it might seem strange to demonstrate 'horse whispering' as a management tool, it is the *essence* of the process that is important. The first skill is to notice how others (human or animal) communicate. Once you know what to pay attention to you can then learn to communicate in their mode, and thus influence their behaviour. Similarly, the more familiar you are with different learning styles and strategies, the better you will be able to enable change.

Learning is about restructuring the meaning of your experience. It is a convergent process in which a mass of information becomes simpler, patterned, and organized. During the time in which your mind is making the necessary connections, you are likely to be in a temporary state of confusion. Although you cannot track the learning process because you do not have direct access to the workings of your mind, you do get the feeling of understanding, that 'Aha!' response as things fall into place, and the confusion disappears. Instead of trying to eliminate confusion from your life, think of it as 'work in progress', a necessary part of learning.

The mind tends to sort information according to familiar patterns. These story and narrative patterns provide useful frameworks for understanding. Creating a story or narrative 'explanation' means that a great deal of information gets deleted. It is easy to select only 'relevant' facts that will fit the structure, and still be convinced that what you have is 'the truth'.

Changing your point of view means that you can perceive alternative versions of what happens. One aim of this book is to show you that having multiple views does not necessarily increase the number of models or story structures you need to know, and to demonstrate that many superficially different interpretations are in fact variations of a few deeper, more general themes. The skill is learning to see beyond the surface details and recognizing the relevant underlying model, paradigm or story. When you do this, you will understand better how other people are perceiving their world, and thus be able to intervene in their stories, in order to effect desirable changes. This means you will have less attachment to any particular explanation or understanding, and greater flexibility in creating and discarding hypotheses according to how useful they are.

This is also a goal of conventional education, though one not usually stated explicitly. The art of learning is finding the principles which you can transfer to your own working style. For example, some of the lessons from horse whispering are:

- Noticing what actually happens in an unfamiliar context requires patient observation, keeping an open mind, and allowing yourself to be confused until you can see the patterns.

- Rapport comes through learning and using someone else's language.

- Trust develops within a relationship which is based on dignity and care.

As Tudor Rickards of Manchester Business School says, 'One of the things that's emphasized in the trust-based horsemanship thing, is that you are trying to learn a language that isn't your language. And I do think too often organizations have people at the top who believe the language of the person at the top is the right language for the organization, rather than "What is the language that my organization understands – and can I learn to speak it?"' (2002).

CURIOSITY

> The desire of knowledge, like the thirst of riches, increases ever with the acquisition of it.
>
> LAURENCE STERNE, *TRISTRAM SHANDY*

Think about your own life, where you have got to, where you want to go. Wherein lies your passion for learning more about yourself, about your world? How committed are you to go on learning? What do you *really* want to know? Ask yourself: 'What am I curious about? What motivates me, drives me to go on learning?'

Curiosity is essential. You ask a question: 'How can I . . . ?', actively seek answers, and do not feel satisfied until your thirst is quenched. During the life of any change project your curiosity will be motivating you to simplify the mass of information by reflecting on what has happened: 'How can I make this simpler? What is really going on here?' and finding ways to organize it into patterns. At other times your curiosity will be driving you into pushing back the boundaries of your ideas, gathering more information: 'What's missing? What else do I need to know?' There will always be more you could find out, but you will be constrained by the time you have available.

LEARNING

> Learning is not something added, but a reorganisation of what already is.
>
> MILTON ERICKSON

Just as teaching is more than simply presenting information to people, so learning is more than just remembering facts. Although you may be inundated by information – news, gossip, internet material – there is no guarantee that your behaviour will change as a result. The second aspect of learning is being able to connect the new information or experience to what you already know.

Learning comes through making connections, forming associations, and creating stories which 'explain' our experience. People feel they understand things when their stories achieve closure. If you are unable to create a meaningful story, the accumulated unconnected facts remain quiz material. The proof of your learning is that you can apply the principles in new situations in order to get the results you want. You also learn to foresee some of the consequences as a logical development of the interventions you choose to make.

'YOU HAVE A LOT TO LEARN'

> One of the signs of a company that doesn't work well is every time a project fails you take heads. Because then no-one ever learns, everyone becomes terribly risk averse, we revert back to 'business as usual.'
>
> REBECCA HENDERSON, EASTMAN KODAK PROFESSOR,
> MASSACHUSSETTS INSTITUTE OF TECHNOLOGY

Learning is ongoing throughout one's career, indeed, for a whole lifetime. However, the word 'learner' often carries limiting or negative associations. For example, as new drivers we hasten to remove the L-plates from our cars as soon as possible. Someone saying 'You have a lot to learn' is probably not just stating a fact, but putting the person down, implying that they are particularly ignorant in some area of life or business and, by contrast, that they are an expert. Learning is mainly associated with school, and for many that was not a good experience. School was something you were 'let out of', as though it were a prison, at the end of the day. Many teachers seemed not to suffer fools gladly, and for the learners it was a hard struggle. Consequently, for some, knowledge of maths or science never developed because of bad feelings associated with poor formal education.

Attitudes towards learning change slowly. The term 'learning' has a disappointing past. Being called 'clever' or 'brainy' is often an insult. In the 1990s, management consultant Graham Robinson encountered the following attitude:

Many of those with whom we spoke became quite visibly uncomfortable whenever the word 'learning' was introduced into the conversation. It appeared that the word was associated with either being a 'learner' or with being 'learned'. In both instances the association tended to be negative rather than positive. . . . Certainly none of the directors involved in our research came anywhere close to echoing the statement made by a Permanent Secretary from one of the major government departments who, in his opening remarks to the participants on a Senior Management Course, commented: 'Quite frankly I would be seriously worried by any manager who, having reached the age of forty, still felt that he had much to learn.'

GRAHAM ROBINSON, 1992: 4

Has this changed? Would the age of 30 now be more appropriate? Has the concept of 'life-long learning' made a difference? Too soon to tell, probably. However, there have been significant moves towards creating learning organizations, which are proving themselves in the marketplace. In order to survive, organizations need to learn. Keith Grint (1997: 88) says: 'Without organizational learning, organizational change is virtually impossible.'

Good teachers inspire us because they are open to learning, and act as role models for being curious. We need teachers to point us in the right direction, to show us what to notice – and then to leave us alone as we make meaning of our experiences. It is only too easy to intervene in the learning process, and deprive the learners of those 'Aha!' moments when the connections are made.

Therefore, if you do not have a clear reason for intervening, restrain your natural impulse to be 'hands on', and allow other people to make 'interesting mistakes'.

LEARNING PROCESSES

Adult learning happens best when there is an *intention* to change, a willingness to perceive the world anew, and some way of incorporating the results of actions taken – feedback from whatever source – into the organization's, and each individual's current 'model of the world'.

The stimuli for learning come from all domains of human experience, not just from the printed word. Learning has been happening throughout your life, mostly out of your awareness, and you are already an expert. For example, you have probably learned to: stand upright, walk, run, dance, read, write and speak one or more languages, play games, make music, drive a car, get your own way with siblings or parents, form relationships, friendships, be a parent and bring up children. Over a lifetime you also learn how to learn, and how you do this will have changed significantly in some areas. Little stays true for all time.

Here are some different kinds of learning:

🔄 **Learning by doing**. The hands-on approach. Training on the job as opposed to academic learning.

🔄 **Rule learning**. Formally by top-down edict or prohibition: 'Thou shalt . . .', 'Thou shalt not . . .'; informally through peer pressure, and social observation, 'The way we do things here'.

🔄 **Fact learning**. Direct scientific observation and through study of texts, reports which are historical, scientific, mathematical and philosophical.

🔄 **Peer learning**. Following fashion, trends, copying others. Ethical and moral learning for maintaining society.

🔄 **Self-directed learning**. Interests, such as hobbies, private research, as an enthusiast.

🔄 **Story learning**. Informally absorbing the ability to know what to do in certain contexts, and to predict outcomes and consequences from understanding intentional behaviour.

🔄 **Spiritual learning**. Comes through self-awareness, self-actualization and moral instruction.

Progress now

Factors for learning

Given your expertise as a learner in each of the above ways, notice which kinds of learning you most enjoy, and identify those factors which reduce or enhance your ability to learn. In your own experience:

- What works well? What promotes good learning?
- What makes learning easy? What inhibits learning?
- Which learning is limited to certain contexts?
- What are your beliefs about learning?
- What are you curious about?

Make a note of your answers; you will explore them in greater detail later in the chapter.

Familiarity with your own learning style enables you to compare and contrast how other people do it. In the following exercises, be curious about the range of variation, and compare your answers with those of your colleagues or friends who are engaged in similar learning processes.

States for learning

Little attention is usually paid to 'What is the best *state* for learning?' 'State' covers your physiological, emotional, mental and spiritual state – all of which vary constantly. You can control your state to a high degree; and you can certainly arrange favourable conditions for the way you learn best.

Progress now

State

Identify your best state for learning: those times when learning is easy, fun, stimulating, and so on. Make a note of what inhibits good learning, and of what works for you,

🔊 **Physiological state:** posture, alignment, symmetry, balance, arousal level, digestion, health, and so on.

Negative (inhibiting):	Positive (enhancing):

🔊 **Emotional and mental state:** your general feeling state (happy, sad, angry, frustrated), and the way you are thinking about the world (beliefs, expectations, attitudes) and so on.

Negative (inhibiting):	Positive (enhancing):

Progress now

Environmental factors

Now consider which of the following environmental factors and conditions enhance your ability to learn. Use these ideas to identify your own preferences.

1. **Location**

   Where do you do your best thinking and learning? Do you prefer to be:

   🖢 Indoors – surrounded by books, gadgets, ideas?

   🖢 Able to access the internet on your computer?

   🖢 Quietly sitting or walking out of doors, in the countryside, in nature?

   🖢 Travelling – while you are commuting, or visiting other countries?

   🖢 In the hustle and bustle of busy places, with music in the background?

   🖢 Surrounded by stimulating things, objects, works or art, architecture?

2. **Space**

   How much space do you need?

🔯   Walk about, pace up and down, or lie on the floor?

🔯   Open spaces, panoramic views, be outdoors?

🔯   'Perspective' so that you can 'stand back' and see your ideas on paper, charts, mind maps™ which are pinned on the wall or whiteboard?

🔯   Physically realized as a three-dimensional model, using figures, objects in a sand tray?

3. Time

🔯   When do you do your best work: are you a morning lark or a night owl?

🔯   For how long can you work effectively? What is the optimum length of time for learning?

4. People

Do you learn best when you are:

🔯   Alone in the quietness of your thoughts, or reading a book in a library, and so forth?

🔯   With other people with whom you can talk, discuss, argue, challenge, get ideas?

This is related to the Introvert/Extrovert dimension: when sorting out a problem, introverts prefer isolation, extroverts seek companionship.

Progress now

Practical changes

Once you have a clear picture of your environmental needs, consider:

🐾 How you could adapt or change your working environment to accommodate these needs.

🐾 How it would be working with people who have different needs.

It may look like chaos – but you may be more creative and productive as a result.

TIME

In Chapter 5 you looked at metaphors for time. How you perceive time will affect your behaviour and how you learn. If you see time as a container waiting to be filled, then you may put a high value on filling it with the highest quality activity. You may want the biggest container possible, in which case, you may choose to work long hours, try to cram everything in (which is often detrimental to quality learning, as there is an imbalance between taking action and taking time to reflect). To some adults, doing nothing is anathema; messing about or just staring out of the window is 'wasting' time. This has given rise to the recent trend in filling their children's time with learning activities.

You know from personal experience that to make connections, you need time to think things through, time to 'sleep on ideas'. Adapting to any change takes some time. Individual needs vary: some people are more reflective and like to think things through; others prefer to be in the thick of things, busily doing several jobs at once.

INFORMATION STRUCTURE

People have preferences for dealing with new information, and how they like to have information presented to them.

Progress now

General preference

Which of the following do you find yourself most drawn to:

Focus on	Motivation
Truths, principles, rules	Authority: Do what is right. Do what you are told. Trust your leader.
Facts, details, logic, strategies	Logic, analysis: Follow procedures. Use proven strategies.
Feelings, values, judgements	Conformity: Demonstrate group norms. Value social approval. Uphold the norms of society.
Ideas, creativity, metaphors	Curiosity: Do your own thing. Be curious. Explore the ramifications.

Which one are you least attracted to or find most challenging? (147)

Learning style preferences

In the lists that follow, decide your own preference for each basic distinction based on how people deal with information. Which do you tend to do more often? There are no right or wrong answers; every option is useful in some context.

To use this as a way of profiling and matching people to jobs, you will need to analyse a job for the preferred criteria. Then you need to assess how closely any person comes to meeting those criteria in the workplace. (Charvet, 1997: 163–170, offers one way of doing this.) For example, a passenger airline pilot needs to follow procedures. Pilots who prefer to do their own thing would do better in a flying circus, without passengers! We probably prefer nurses who are more oriented towards other people than focused on themselves.

You may have different preferences for work and home contexts: 'In this situation [at work] I would tend to do X, but in other situations [at home] I usually do Y.' Many people have this split between the personal and the professional parts of their lives, and do not transfer skills across contexts. For example, you may be an excellent manager at work, handling a number of energetic employees or colleagues, but feel overwhelmed at home with your children!

Progress now

Sensory preference

Although you use all your senses in your interactions with the world, you may develop a preference for communicating with other people in terms of:

- **Visual.** Seeing things, in writing, or in pictures or diagrams. 'A picture speaks a thousand words.' You like to meet people face to face, observe their non-verbal cues and size them up.

- **Auditory.** Listening to what others tell you, as there is a great deal you can learn from the tonality and inflection of the voice – the 'real message' is in the way they say things. You may spend a lot of time on the phone.

- **Kinesthetic.** You like to touch other people, and are happy to touch people as part of your work. You gather information about others, provide support and encouragement through touch. You enjoy 'getting your hands dirty,' or adopt a 'hands-on' approach to get the feel of equipment or technology. You understand a product by handling it, playing with it, getting a feel for it.

Progress now

Structure preferences

There are several aspects of structure which affect how you process information. You could become confused if you are given information in a non-preferred way. Notice which of the following make learning and comprehension easier.

1 Amount

How much do you want at any one time? Do you like to have one fact or idea and deal with that, and then move on to the next; or do you like everything at once and then sort it out?

2 Level

How much detail do you want to begin with?

🔖 With new information, do you first want to know the context, the big picture, before you get the details; or do you prefer to build your understanding from the ground up?

🔖 If you prefer the overview first, you could be irritated if someone supplies you with endless details, and urge them to 'Get to the point!'

3 Order and connectedness

As information arrives, it needs to be sorted and structured. This is usually easier if the information is presented logically. However, if you assume that the arrival sequence is the 'correct' one, this could inhibit you from finding alternative ways of understanding the message.

🖎 **Sequential.** You like things already arranged logically so that you can follow the argument. You resent having to backtrack to restructure your understanding.

🖎 **Random**, as it comes. You enjoy the challenge of sorting the information, of making connections, and of patterning disparate facts, as this triggers further interesting ideas.

4 Divergent/convergent

This distinction relates to two aspects of learning:

🖎 **Divergent.** You want to be creative, increase options, widen the range of activities. To maintain this larger vision, you strive to keep things open as long as possible so that you can continue to make new connections.

🖎 **Convergent.** You want to make things conform to set standards, narrow the options, reduce variability, the number of unknowns. In so doing you reduce the mass of information by setting a frame, defining the elements, tying up loose ends.

For example, do you choose work projects which you already know a lot about, or do you prefer to explore the unknown? In your social life, do you choose your friends according to whether they inspire and challenge you, or do you prefer those who maintain the status quo?

Managing change requires both convergent and divergent thinking at different times. You start by exploring possibilities, but then condense your ideas into a manageable form – the vision – which other people will then expand and implement in various ways.

5 Procedures/options

When do you conform to group norms or conventions, and when do you feel free to follow your own inclinations? Following accepted procedures is 'safe,' and may save time. You also need to express your creativity and find innovative ways of doing things. Do you treat instructions as 'commands' or 'suggestions'?

- ✒ **Procedures.** You prefer to follow tried and tested methods, do as you are told, obey the rules.

- ✒ **Options.** You prefer to improvise, do your own thing, try out new ideas, avoid repeating yourself.

6 Validity

What source of information do you rely on? What influences your choice of technological products such as phones or computers, or personal items such as shoes or clothing?

- ✒ **Self.** Own wisdom. You make a decision based on personal knowledge or judgement.

- ✒ **Other.** You seek out expert advice, or you ask your friends and colleagues what they do. To what extent are you influenced by peer group preferences?

>   **Neutral or 'Objective'.** You consult reference databases, consumer 'best buy' guides.
>
> **7   Evidence requirements**
>
> The amount of evidence you need to feel secure in your decision depends on:
>
>   The number of examples.
>
>   The number of times you are exposed to the information.
>
>   The period of time that has to pass.
>
> **8   Self/other orientation**
>
> Your primary consideration is:
>
>   Self-interest, benefit: 'What's in it for me?'
>
>   Other people come first.

The purpose of these 'Progress now' exercises is that you learn to recognize patterns in human behaviour. As a result, you will be better able to match other people's styles and get better rapport with them. Another benefit is that the greater your understanding of the range of possibilities, the more you can get out of life, in terms of work, relationships and leisure activities.

CHAPTER 7
Models for Understanding

It is the theory that determines what we can observe.

EINSTEIN'S REMARK TO HEISENBERG

Without theory, experience has no meaning.
Without theory, one has no questions to ask.
Hence without theory there is no learning.

W. EDWARDS DEMING

ANOTHER WORLD

We interpret new information in terms of our existing understanding of the world. Arie de Geus (1997: 41) tells the story of a tribal chief's visit to Singapore. At the beginning of the twentieth century some British explorers encountered a tribal chief in an isolated part of the Malayan peninsula. Although the tribe lived in a pre-technological culture, the highly intelligent chief had a deep understanding of that world. As an experiment, the explorers decided to take him into the bustling seaport of Singapore, already a complex society and market economy, enjoying overseas trade. The city had multi-storey buildings and a harbour with big ships. They toured the chief around the city for a day, submitting him to thousands of signals of potential change for his own society. Returning to his mountain valley, they debriefed him: 'What was the most exciting, the most interesting thing you have seen?' And he thought for a while, and then told them of the only thing that seemed important: he had seen a man carrying more bananas on his head than he had ever thought one man could carry!

We need frameworks and models for interpreting experience. Without them you literally cannot see what is there. Even people from advanced technological societies visiting so-called 'primitive' cultures are unable to perceive what the natives pay attention to. It takes time to learn about 'alien' social structure and customs. You might think of Australian Aborigines as inhabiting a bleak, featureless, sandy terrain – until you learn to see the outback through their eyes. Roy Disney (Walt Disney's nephew, who worked as an assistant film editor) says about Disney's natural history film, *The Living Desert*:

> . . . most people drive through the desert, or ride the train through the desert, and they look out there and there's nothing! And to have pointed out to them all the things that really do exist in this what appears to be a dead wilderness, was really a big revelation.

The environment is 'nothing' only when you cannot make the appropriate distinctions. It 'lives' when we have patterns and paradigms for understanding. As children we are shown what to pay attention to, and learn to name what we perceive. This happens formally in our educational system, and informally all the time as we strive to comprehend the unfamiliar. We develop our 'models of the world' by generalizing from the experiences life offers us.

ORGANIZING PRINCIPLES

In many contexts, the organizing principles are not and need not be made explicit. You probably only become aware of your own models when someone else 'violates' them, for example, by using 'inappropriate' language or dress code. Caught out, they justify their behaviour: 'That's how *I* learned to do it.' A model or theory helps you perceive what is otherwise invisible. On the whole, when things are working well, you do not need a theory. It is when things are *not* working and you are not getting the changes you want that you do need to understand what is happening.

The model of change described in this book enables you to deal with the practical aspects of managing change. It is very general and has wide application. Other people need not know the organizing principles of your thinking. Using the model may seem familiar, as it is in accord with a deep pattern of everyday life. Your skill comes in being able to apply the model in different contexts.

Chapter 1 introduced the I–R–T Model (Figure 1.1) as a way of distinguishing kinds of change. This general pattern has many interpretations. One is that we make different *kinds* of changes, and these can be represented on different levels. We can also relate these levels to the distinctions between body, mind and spirit. The term 'mind' refers to all thinking activities, how we make sense of the world; the term 'spirit' is an inexact term referring to that which is 'beyond words'.

Table 7.1 Making connections

T: Transform	Spirit	Spirituality – being	Level III
R: Reform	Mind	Cognition – thinking	Level II Four Realities Model
I: Inform	Body	Physiology – doing	Level I

The I–R–T model can be expanded into a more comprehensive model that covers the range of changes we are interested in.

We can represent models graphically, using diagrams, charts and maps. Any representation symbolizes only those aspects which are relevant for your purposes. The meaning of a diagram comes from interpreting the words or symbols and the relationships between them. Figure 7.1 shows a metaphorical landscape in which change takes place and relates to the patterns of change described in this book. Some of these changes are diagrammed in Figure 8.1 (page 199). The following interpretation of this diagram is in terms of different points of view, referred to as 'Perceptual Positions'.

The lower level stays the same, and covers non-verbal states and behaviours. The cognitive middle level is subdivided into four types. You have already met these four categories under many different names – both in your life and in this book. The upper level also stays the same and includes that which is 'beyond words'. If you were to turn this diagram into a cylinder by joining the top and bottom edges, this would indicate a continuity between Levels I and III, the sense of switching off language and 'just being' in the world.

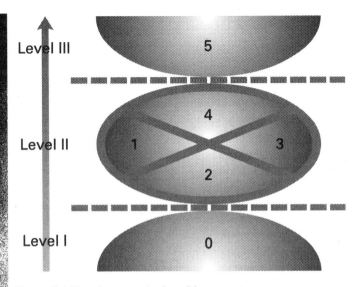

Level III

Level II

Level I

Figure 7.1 The six perceptual positions

THE SIX PERCEPTUAL POSITIONS MODEL

The Perceptual Position model proposes six fundamentally different ways of perceiving the world.

Table 7.2 The Six Perceptual Positions model

0 **Zeroth** **Position**	**Doing. Physiology, 'just doing'** Habitual action. Often in a trance-like state as when you are totally engrossed in physical activity, or 'running on automatic' having 'switched off your thinking'. Be aware of this if you are designing spaces for crowds of people in public spaces, shops, or at sporting events.
1 **First** **Position**	**Truth. Defining, discriminating** The way things are. Being yourself, at home in the familiar 'here and now' world, aware of what you are doing, thinking and feeling. Perceiving the world 'as it is', supported by your beliefs about what is true.
2 **Second** **Position**	**Alternatives. Analysing, sequencing** The way to do things. Seeing things from other people's points of view, modelling their way of doing and thinking. Realizing there are many ways of experiencing the world, and alternative courses of action that get results.

3 **Third** **Position**	**Values. Judging, evaluating, deciding** The way we do things. Observing your experience by 'stepping back'. Thinking *about* experience, taking responsibility for it, evaluating your feelings, prioritizing your actions, and deciding what to do. Ensuring that your behaviour honours your own values, and those of the society or group you belong to.	
4 **Fourth** **Position**	**Ideas. Connecting, creating, exploring** The way things could be. Imagining possibilities. The 'creative self' which 'reinvents' your reality, recodes your experience by reframing your perceptions, invents new metaphors by making new connections.	
5 **Fifth** **Position**	**Being. Accepting, 'universal', 'in the zone'** Losing your sense of individuality; being 'at one' with the universe, experiencing a 'universal' connection. Sometimes a quiet, reflective state achieved through ritual, meditation, or feeling awe-inspired by nature or human achievement. At other times an ironic sense of the universe being totally arbitrary, 'all made up'.	

Progress now

Adopting different points of view

Personal change happens when you shift your point of view to a different perceptual position. People differ in how well they make such mental shifts, and in their willingness to do so. Having the ability to see an issue from someone else's point of view – through their eyes – means that you temporarily 'become a different person' by adopting an alternative set of cultural or perceptual beliefs.

For example, consider how the act of making and drinking a cup of tea varies in the following cultures: English, French, American, Arabic, Indian and Japanese. The significance of the act depends upon each culture's belief systems, cultural norms, social customs, and so forth.

CHANGING PERCEPTUAL POSITIONS

The Perceptual Positions model proposes that change is essentially about moving from one perceptual position to another. For example, to 'pay attention' means moving from Level I (0) to Level II (1–4), and becoming aware of what you are doing. Many simple changes involve a single move from one perceptual position to another. The 'Progress now' above requires a move from First to Second Position.

Many management techniques involve a series of such moves, visiting several perceptual positions in turn (see McWhinney *et al*, 1997). One familiar sequence of changes involves cycling around the four positions on Level II. Sometimes called 'The Hero's Journey', this is a common theme in our cultural stories, and the basic structure of many Hollywood movies (Vogler, 1998; Young 2001: 190). The final transition, from 4 back to 1, which represents returning home after the adventure, is occasionally included, for example, in *The Wizard of Oz*.

THE LEADER'S JOURNEY

Another cyclic journey, $1 \rightarrow 4 \rightarrow 3 \rightarrow 2$, which Will McWhinney (1997: 125) refers to as the 'Path of Revitalization', I call 'The Leader's Journey', and it underpins the thinking in this book. The starting point is the clarification of the new vision or truth which the change manager wishes to bring into reality. This is why Chapter 3 focused on the role of the individual who is leading the change, and explored the first two stages, First and Fourth. Third and Second Positions are more about management and groups. UMIST (University of Manchester Institute of Science and Technology) professor Cyril Levicki says: 'Leaders don't manage and managers don't lead. . . . All managers, ultimately, have somebody above them to take responsibility for some or most aspects of their role for the organization. . . . It is only the leader who bears total responsibility for all facets of the organization's future and its results' (2002: 2–3).

First Position

This journey starts by imagining how the present reality could be improved. Leaders do a great deal of preliminary work in creating their vision of the new state of the world, using 'What if?' scenarios to explore the implications. You must believe in this vision, and therefore it has to be rich in detail, and offer something that you and others will emotionally engage with. If you do not care, then why should anyone else want to commit to it? To win the hearts and minds of the people you want to join with you, this vision must be more than a few vague, positive-sounding slogans.

First to Fourth

Simply having a vision does not get things moving. Products do not sell themselves. Any new product, idea or vision needs someone to publicly promote its benefits. Your job, as change manager, is to descend the mountain with your vision, your tablets of stone, and disseminate this 'truth' to the project team, and thus unite and motivate them into making it real. One way of influencing people is by using Fourth Position's metaphors and stories. You will come across as authentic and convincing the more you can live in the world of your story. This means seeing the project unfold in detail, seeing yourself doing what needs to be done, adapting constantly as you progress, until you achieve some kind of completion.

Fourth to Third

Your vision is only a title or synopsis of what you want to happen; the rest of the story is waiting to be told. Your audience will make connections between your metaphor and the future reality. A powerful story, expressed in rich, captivating, sensory-based words, will engage the feelings and values of Third Position. Motivate others to commit to the project by explaining the benefits of the proposed change. Appeal to the highest values of all involved, and include their self-interest – what's in it for them.

Storytelling is a shared experience which brings people together, and aligns their thinking towards a shared goal. It should be fun. Although you might think that telling stories is unusual, most people are actually doing this informally a great deal of the time. When you meet with your friends, do you not recount the stories of recent events: about your holiday, about the big match, or the latest political scandal? You are a storyteller.

Third to Second

Only when you have everyone 'on board' – committed and facing the same direction – do you start the project rolling in a practical sense. Second Position is analytical and strategic, and requires the allocation of specific roles and tasks to the project team. Each person needs to know exactly what they have to do. The change manager's role now consists of:

- ◊ Providing guidelines. Giving the big picture – the overall vision.

- ◊ Defining boundaries. Every project has limits, and everyone needs to know where the boundaries are. How far does this project extend; what is included, what is not? As the project progresses there may be a need to reset the boundaries in the light of experience. Keeping everyone informed all the time is vital.

- ◊ Setting targets. Establishing criteria to recognize when you have achieved your aim.

- ◊ Allocating specific work role details to individuals or work groups, and explaining how the team members are expected to work together: who relates to whom?

- ◊ Clarifying confusion. Arranging for mediation should disputes arise.

You have now done a major part of the work. The idea is to set things up so that they run smoothly. The actual project becomes more about *steering* the group towards the goal. You may want to delegate this task to someone else if 'project management mode' is not your primary skill. They will refer those decisions which have a bearing on the initial vision to you for your interpretation. You need to retain sight of the project, or it is likely to get out of control.

Second to First

Noticing what happens and monitoring feedback are vital and ongoing activities throughout the change process. Are you on track? Is what you achieved in accord with your vision? Because your purpose is defined, you can measure the success of the project by comparing the dream with the reality. Ideally the successful completion of the task will reinforce the original vision; the evidence may often be the bottom line: 'Did we make a profit?'

You need all the sensory awareness you can muster to notice what is actually going on. This is no time for self-delusion or for Pollyanna thinking that everything is wonderful because you had a dream. Stay open to information from your own senses (you have to be totally involved), and from other people who are going to be telling you things which are 'good' and 'bad'. Insist they tell you the 'bad' news, because knowing when you are off course means you can take corrective action. Adopt the attitude that this is just information which is helping you to become closer to your vision – as long as you are willing to amend, update or even choose a new vision.

Remember that no project is about an ultimate truth; it is about getting something to work. If you get stuck, shift your perception of the issues, and be a role model of change for others – which is what learning is about, after all!

Complete each journey by celebrating your successes. Maximize the learning from a project by taking time out to reflect on what happened (this is covered in Chapter 10). Notice what needs to be done next. No change project results in total happiness for everyone; no solution is perfect. It is simply a step closer, and time to begin planning the next change. Things will be different, so assume the unexpected, and be ready for a challenge to what you have just learned. Nothing new there!

PREFERENCES

Although people are continually shifting their point of view, they will have a preference for a particular mode of perception. With practice you may recognize 'where someone else is coming from' by paying attention to what they say, the way they behave, and so on. This is useful information for building rapport with them, and for finding appropriate ways of shifting their stuck thinking that limits them because they cannot conceive of any alternatives. Therefore, as an enabler of change, you have to decide:

- Where is this person currently? How are they stuck?
- Where is a good place for them to shift to?
- What is a good way of doing that? What do I need to say? What do I need to get them to do? What do I need to suggest they think about?

Zero and Five – the non-linguistic states of being

Each position has its own characteristic ways of behaving and thinking. Moving to Zeroth Position means shifting your attention away from thinking about things and engaging your body's physiology. For example, under stress, people often stop breathing; taking a breath re-establishes their ability to act appropriately. Engaging in physical movement or exercise changes someone's emotional state, and enlivens their attention so that you can communicate with them more fully.

Fifth position is similar in some ways, which is why in Figure 7.1 (p. 160) the extremes are represented as semi-circles. The difference between the physical and the spiritual is fuzzy; they both involve switching off the internal chatter of the mind. Taking a moment for silent contemplation — expanding the mind to fill the universe — can change your state even more than jumping up and down. Rituals and meditations may have a powerful effect on individuals and groups. Would you want to use some kind of ritual process at the beginning and ending of your team meetings? If you are congruent about this, you will often find willing participants who appreciate the changes it brings.

THE FOUR POSITIONS ON LEVEL II

These four cognitive positions are frequently interpreted in terms of personality characteristics – ways of perceiving the world each of which focuses on different aspects of experience. I refer to these as the *Four Reality modes* or types. There is a strong connection between the Perceptual Positions Model and the Four Realities Model; they are different manifestations of the same deep structure which appears in many different forms in our culture.

A theoretical basis for this fourfold pattern

This fourfold schema has been described by Will McWhinney (1997: 27), and the communication implications explored in Young (2001). It is based on two dimensions *Monistic–Pluralistic* and *Determined–Free Will* (Table 7.3).

Combining these into a 2×2 grid produces four *types* or *reality modes*. McWhinney names the 'pure' types: *Unitary*, *Sensory*, *Social* and *Mythic*, and I shall be using these terms. An indication of what each type pays attention to is given in the four boxes (Table 7.3). Each person tends towards one of these modes of thinking – their preference for their 'model of reality'.

Table 7.3 The Four Realities

	Monistic – One	Pluralistic – Many
Determined	**Unitary U Defining**	**Sensory Se Sequencing**
	🔃 Truths	🔃 Behaviours
	🔃 Policies	🔃 Facts
	🔃 Principles	🔃 Data
	🔃 Rules	🔃 Logic
Free Will	**Mythic M Connecting**	**Social So Evaluating**
	🔃 Visions	🔃 Feelings
	🔃 Ideas	🔃 Values
	🔃 Metaphors	🔃 Preferences
	🔃 Opportunities	🔃 Judgements

Recognizing the four types

Many personality profiling instruments detail four or more distinct types. Many fit this model well; others use different dimensions. The names are those used by Will McWhinney (McWhinney 1997: 27). People are not 'pure' types, but a mixture of all four in different proportions. Here are some indicators of the characteristics for each mode of thinking.

Unitary – First Position

Unitary mode people actively engage with the present. The positive type is the strong, principled leader, who acts purposefully, according to the rules. The negative type is the authoritarian personality, the despot, unwilling to consider other points of view. They have to be 'right', blame others for mistakes, and try to eliminate dissenters. They expect the world to revolve around them: everything must be done immediately; subordinates must heed their bidding and comply.

Thinking 'This is how it is' limits their vision. They become stuck having no alternatives. Taking language literally, assuming words have correct meanings, defined in dictionaries, encourages people to 'fix' the world. They may be deficient in the sense of humour department, lacking the flexibility of thought required for changing perceptual frames.

Conflict arises when different unitary models of the world clash: 'I'm right and you're wrong!' It may require much effort to get opposing parties to realize that truths are not absolute. Ask them to consider alternative points of view: 'How would So-and-so think of this?', 'What would your boss do in this situation?' and so on.

Sensory – Second Position

Sensory mode people are more analytical and concerned with how things happen over time. They are often described as scientific as they require sensory-based evidence and logical rigour. They tend to be practical planners, people who can engineer ideas into reality. They often go into great detail, compile lists, develop efficient strategies, based on logical decision making – *Star Trek*'s Mr Spock. Linguistically they may have 'swallowed the dictionary': 'The disparate alternatives necessitate meticulous deliberation before an expedient resolution can be promulgated.' They may be aloof and unemotional, living in a world of facts and theories. To others they seem unfeeling, making decisions from the head rather than from the heart.

They are good at seeing things from an 'objective' point of view and are often keen to argue anything by taking a contrary position. Anyone in sales or the caring professions needs to have a facility for Second Position, seeing the world from their customer or client's point of view. Personal Assistants need to cultivate the ability to anticipate the needs of their boss, and prepare things without being asked.

Social – Third Position

Social mode people show a concern for the feelings of the group or society, ensuring that the needs of everyone are being met, that balance is maintained, and that ethical and moral standards are being upheld. They tend to think about what is important, evaluate what is happening. They prefer conformity, doing what is socially acceptable. They feel that they ought to include others, and prevent them from 'rocking the boat'. One concern is for justice and fairness for all. Linguistically, they use 'oughts' and 'shoulds' in order to keep themselves and others in line with the norms of the group. They are 'people-people' – often caring and sociable team-players, who look after the group and keep everyone happy. The negative aspect is when they act emotionally, illogically and irrationally, and attempt to placate anyone who has higher status. A common difficulty is getting these kinds of people to work to Sensory mode targets, prepare budgets, carry out controlled trials, and understand the need for presenting a case that accountants appreciate.

Mythic – Fourth Position

Mythic mode people are creative thinkers who use their imagination to explore new ideas and expand visions of what might be. They like to develop theories of how things work, and think into the future by contemplating options and opportunities, and follow the ramifications of ideas. They are the artists, the dreamers, the visionaries who see things in terms of patterns, metaphors and symbols. They see connections between ideas, and explore the possibilities by asking: 'What if . . . ?' Full of ideas, they may seem to be living on a different planet, and have to be brought back to earth in order to begin the practical implementation of their dreams.

The positive aspect of Mythic mode is the creative and witty ideas person. Everything can be 'interesting' and they get very enthusiastic for short periods. The negative aspects appear in the bored or distracted jokester whom no one finds funny, or the person who seems to be in an imaginary world of their own and who needs to be grounded by asking for workable solutions or practical applications. Linguistically they may have a very inventive use of words, making puns and jokes, and be adept at creating neologisms, metaphors and analogies.

Progress now

What's missing?

The differences between these four types are deeply embedded in our personalities, and revealed in our preferences and tendencies for thinking and acting in any given situation. Practically, it may be more useful to know which reality mode is *under-represented*. Notice which way of thinking or behaving you do the least; prefer not to do; or have difficulty understanding. For example:

- 🍃 (U) Being assertive, expressing a vision, being clear about how things are, enforcing the rules.

- 🍃 (Se) Using logical analysis, mathematics, finance, the physical sciences and technology.

- 🍃 (So) Getting on with other people, socializing, networking, joining groups, having many friends.

- 🍃 (M) Being creative, artistic, an ideas person; seeing beneath the surface, making connections; doing your own thing, making jokes.

This should indicate which aspects of life need boosting in order to create more balance. It will also point to any imbalance in a project team.

MANNER OF CHANGE

Each type has a preferred style for making changes:

🕉 **Unitary:** Impose their truth or vision on others, by order or decree. They expect obedience, conformity, with everyone following the rules.

🕉 **Sensory:** Test their theories, investigate and analyse the evidence. They employ objective tests, and rely on statistical results and probability estimates.

🕉 **Social:** Unite people in productive teams, which develop strong norms and a clear moral code. Individuals should act according to shared values and what is in the group's best interests.

🕉 **Mythic:** Use unconventional methods, provide experiences that allow opportunities for exploring creativity – just to see what happens. They brainstorm to discover new and exciting ideas.

Challenging each mode

You can instigate reform-type changes by challenging the thinking or criteria for the particular mode. For example, you could suggest changing:

- **U**.The rules, the current truth. Ask: 'Has this always been true?', 'Who told you this?'

- **Se**.The process, sequence of steps. Ask: 'How else could this be achieved?', How would your client perceive this?'

- **So**.The values, the priorities. Ask: 'What matters? What is important?', 'Is everyone agreed on this?'

- **M**.The metaphors, story, meaning. Ask: 'What are the consequences of this?', How else might this turn out?', or ask: 'What would be a different metaphor for this?'

USING THE MODEL

The two cyclic patterns – *Hero's Journey* and the *Leader's Journey* – are deeply embedded in our culture, and underpin the stories we use to explain experience. Communicating your ideas using such basic story structures will match how other people think and will 'makes sense' at a deep level. Recognizing these patterns means you can use them to your advantage. The more abstract a model or paradigm is, the more widely you can apply it. However, the patterns are rarely made explicit, and it requires practice to recognize them under layers of detail.

Use stories to communicate your vision, to spread understanding of how things are now and how they could be in the future. However, a convincing story does not necessarily have a greater truth-value; nor is it the final word on any experience. A film-editor is limited to working with the actual film shot, but can still re-edit what there is and, by restructuring the story, change its meaning and effect. Similarly, you cannot change your actual experiences, but you still have the power to change your interpretation of events and see things afresh. Change is frequently about reperceiving the stories you use to understand your life.

MOVING FROM THINKING TO MAKING IT HAPPEN

The Perceptual Positions Model provides a useful way of understanding how change works, and the Four Realities model suggests 'where people are coming from', and how to intervene for maximum effect. A theoretical model empowers you to find many ways of manifesting the general principles to meet the needs of different contexts. The concept of shifting points of view guides you in developing appropriate interventions to get the changes you want. By thinking through the likely consequences you can prepare for several contingencies: 'A Third Position response would be of this nature; a Mythic response would be . . .', and so on.

The next chapter suggests some practical ways of using these theories in leading a change project.

CHAPTER 8
Action

The world can only be grasped by action, not by contemplation. The hand is more important than the eye. . . . The hand is the cutting edge of the mind.

BRONOWSKI, 1973

Fennyman: So what do we do?
Henslowe: Nothing. Strangely enough, it all turns out well
Fennyman: How?
Henslowe: I don't know. It's a mystery.

NORMAN AND STOPPARD,
SHAKESPEARE IN LOVE, 1999: 23

GETTING BETTER AT CHANGING

If you could achieve your desired change by yourself, you would probably already have done so. Change is a group effort; members contribute according to their expertise. Therefore, whatever the change project, a major part is developing your people skills: 'winning hearts and minds', getting people 'on your side', 'aligned', getting 'team players' working together towards achieving the vision.

Change leaders are neither issued with magic wands, nor do they have all the answers. Be honest; set a frame by explaining: 'First of all let me tell you what I can and can't do for you. What I can do is create the best conditions for achieving our aims. But I cannot wave a magic wand and miraculously cure all the world's problems. However, I do believe that we have the resources for working together to make this project succeed.'

CONTEXT

The context of change encompasses physical, social, cultural, and metaphorical environments: the 'lay of the land', 'where people are coming from'. Because you will become part of that context, you need to understand the culture or worldview of the people involved, in order to know how best to fit in. Start from where they are rather than tread on dreams, ignite feelings, violate values, and so on. Rarely do people appreciate 'outsiders' coming in and violating their group norms by imposing changes to 'the way we do things around here'. Find out what is true, consult like mad, adapt yourself and adopt their metaphorical reality.

COERCIVE CHANGE

Sometimes change is thrust upon you: 'Change or else!' Being forced to behave differently is a pattern familiar in childhood. You are surrounded by parents, teachers and other powerful people who assume they know what is best for you. Becoming a teenager is a transition point, where you assert your own desires. Adulthood is less hot-headed, and people are willing to take time and effort to influence others for mutual benefit.

However strong your desire to get results, you will be successful only to the extent that others join with you. Communicating ideas 'by decree' inevitably mismatches their worldview, and they probably will not understand what you are talking about. If others cannot see the value of the proposed change to them or to their customers, or imagine how it could be accomplished, you run the (high) risk of losing support, cooperation and goodwill. The superficial compliance hides underlying resentment, and the change you will effect is people choosing to be elsewhere as soon as possible.

BEING A ROLE MODEL

A successful change manager inspires others by being a role model of curiosity, flexibility and openness. You need to be accepting of other people's ideas. You do not necessarily have to do what they say, but you should explore their ideas for possible benefits. Of course, they may be offering solutions to a different problem, in which case, thank them and encourage them to come up with further ideas.

Humility is a vital quality. Lower your status by admitting that you cannot solve the other person's problem for them, and empower them to take more responsibility for their own learning. Personal change and learning takes time, and does not thrive when you charge in and try to *fix* things. 'Fix' has ambiguous meanings: 'to mend' and 'to set solid'. Understand the metaphorical reality: if people are *stuck*, they are already *fixed* in their thinking, so you need to do something different. Thinking that people are 'broken' is not an appropriate attitude for a change manager. If people are confused or lost they need guidance. In your role as mentor or coach, you are helping everyone to achieve their best by developing their own resources. People are usually happy to change if they have the information necessary for making the appropriate decisions.

RAPPORT AT EVERY STAGE

Establishing and maintaining rapport is a learnable skill. Metaphorically you start living inside someone else's model of the world to find out how it works. By matching their behaviour and thinking at all levels you will gain insights into their needs, wants, outcomes, attitudes, and so on. As people are not usually aware of this information, they will not perceive you as doing anything untoward. They are more likely to feel acknowledged, valued, and will perceive you as 'one of us'.

You can match other people in terms of:

- **Physiology.** Posture, gestures, speed of moving, rhythms, energy level, and so on.

- **Communication style.** How they speak: the actual words, their jargon and specific content; the speed, rhythm and tonality they use, and so on.

- **Reality model.** To influence other people, you need a good idea of 'where they are coming from': how they perceive their world, their preferences, beliefs and values. Develop your awareness of these four different ways of perceiving the world (see Chapter 7) so that you can match those ways of being.

> **Culture.** The evidence of a culture comes in the superficial aspects of life: decor, clothing, fashion, jargon, and so on: 'How they do things here.' It also helps to recognize the metaphorical construction they use (covered in Chapter 5). Consider also the mindset, way of thinking of their end-users, or customers who are going to benefit from the change project.

> **Status and power relationships.** Within any existing group you also need to know: who is boss; what is the pecking order, the status hierarchy. Although you are nominally the leader, coming in from the outside and usurping power from the actual group leader will create resentment. You want the group leader on your side.

MOTIVATIONAL CHANGE

Only when you have rapport with your team do you explain your vision to them. Prepare several versions of your story that will match the particular values and preferences of the group you are with. Organize your material to include:

- *Who* you are, and *who else* is involved.

- *Why* this change now. What is at stake? Be honest. State what the current problem is, and what kind of solution would be appropriate. Tell people how they will benefit (if they won't benefit, why are you doing this?).

- *What* you intend to do: the context and boundaries of the project; the overarching principles; the intended outcome.

- *How* you intend to implement a solution, the overall strategy, the particular methods; who will be doing which job; how long will it take?

- *When* you expect to see results.

- The expected consequences and opportunities that this change will open up.

GATHERING INFORMATION

Asking questions is a good way to find out where you are starting from. However, questioning is neither totally 'neutral' nor totally 'non-directive'; you make the difference. The kinds of questions you ask indicate what you consider important, and will direct the other person's attention to what they should be aware of. Notice the effect your questions have on the other person, and pay attention to how they respond to you. Allow them time to think, time to search for answers. Use a relaxed, 'soft-eyed' manner to notice the non-verbal responses: changes in breathing, skin colour, muscle movements around the eyes and around the mouth, etc.

How much information do you need? What is sufficient? You could gather information for ever and still not be satisfied. However, if you are going to get things done, there comes a time when you must accept that you have to work with what you have – accept that it is partial, biased or ambiguous, because it comes from other human beings who have their preferences, points of view and communication difficulties, just as you do.

Progress now

No project starts from scratch. Everyone comes with a wagon-load of experience, skills, know-how – so acknowledge this. Ask people about their expertise and find out about existing resources. You need to know about the group's mind-set. What do they pay attention to? Which reality mode, thinking mode, problem mode do they prefer? What are they good at? How do they excel? Here are some questions to ask:

- ✑ 'What are the rules – formal and informal – for this group/organization?'
- ✑ 'What are your expectations?'
- ✑ 'What are the shared values of the group?
- ✑ 'How do you see yourselves metaphorically?'

Find ways of eliciting the generic, transferable skills relevant to this project. In some cultures the question 'What are you good at?' is not often asked.

- ✑ 'What resources, skills, knowledge, expertise do you need?'
- ✑ 'What skills do you have?'

🔃 'Which kinds of problem are you good at solving? How specifically do you do that?'

🔃 'What have you already tried which didn't work?', 'How else could you do this?'

🔃 'How do you usually go about solving these kinds of problem?'

What is their attitude towards change and learning?

🔃 'How do you learn from experience?'

🔃 'How do you ensure that the learning is passed to others?'

🔃 'Is there any history of unresolved issues with this group?'

To whom do they turn when they are having difficulties? Are they willing to 'buy in' outside help, or do they think they can solve this 'in-house'?

🔃 'Where do you get your ideas from? Who has been a major influence in the way you think?

🔃 'Who are your models of excellence? Who inspires you?'

Notice which metaphorical descriptions are used as these could provide clues about what needs to change. Unravelling the knots could mean unpicking the narrative threads in use within that culture.

COMMUNICATION SKILLS

Good communication does not mean sending e-mails to all and sundry, or simply telling them: 'It's on the website.' Many people already suffer from information overload; yet another e-mail could be an excuse for switching off. There is no shortage of facts; what is often needed is an *interpretation* of those facts, and help in understanding the implications of what they mean. Therefore, help others integrate *your* vision into *their* understanding by translating the 'facts' into their preferred mode. For example, some people quickly get the picture; others like the sound of what you are saying; some feel deeply about your message; and a proportion think in abstract concepts. Cover all possibilities by using plenty of sensory-based *see*, *hear* and *feel* words. If you talk in abstracts, people will envision something, but it is unlikely to resemble what you have in mind.

Use positive language to say what you want, rather than what you do not want. One driving school uses the slogan, 'We won't fail you.' So what do you think about? Failing! It would be better to refer to success!

Utter seriousness could indicate a lack of flexibility; stay light, make your communications about change fun. This does not mean putting clip-art on your memos. Genuine excitement and enthusiasm will show through in how you express yourself.

Help others to assess what is important and point out what they need to pay attention to, what will be different as a result, and what changes they should expect. Supply the criteria they need to be able to notice changes: 'Pay attention to the sound of the engine. Notice when the pitch changes to a steady tone, because this is a good indicator of things working well. If it starts to whine, it is unbalanced, and the likely consequence is a breakdown.'

WORKING WITH METAPHORS

A huge amount of information is available on problem solving in objective disciplines such as engineering, architecture, accountancy, technology and all kinds of science. There is far less about how to change mind-sets, perception and under-standing. You can help people shift their point of view using metaphors offered by the Perceptual Positions Model with everyday phrases such as 'helicopter vision'; 'If I were in your shoes . . .' or 'I'd love to be a fly on the wall . . .'.

METAPHORS OF NOT CHANGING

People prefer living in a relatively stable world of consistency and continuity. When you forget how creative and flexible you can be, you get 'stuck' – in First Position – as if you were in a box or restricted space, with no way out, no idea how to move. Therefore, anything that shifts your perception, gets you to adopt another point of view, will generate change. The art is in finding ways to challenge stuckness and offer acceptable alternatives.

DEALING WITH RESISTANCE

'Resistance' is a metaphor applied to those not wishing to move or change. Many management books list ways of dealing with and overcoming resistance, inertia, confusion, being stuck, and so forth. Our urge to remedy situations leads to the danger of rushing in and trying to change other people without first understanding how they are stuck. In Chapter 4 you looked at how you identify and move through your own kinds of resistance. Similar processing is needed when you want to help others move on. At a cognitive level, change necessitates restructuring subjective experience. Moving someone from 'stuck' to anywhere else will have a profound effect. Figure 8.1 shows a range of movements from First Position, based on the Perceptual Positions Model.

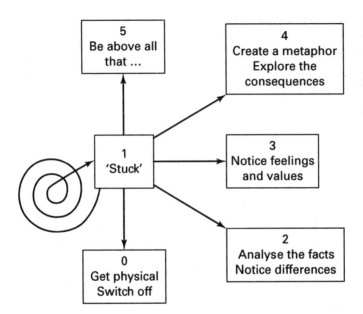

Figure 8.1 Six choices

DIFFICULT PEOPLE

Everybody is somebody's 'difficult person'.

ACLAND, 1995: 159

When you are dealing with people who are difficult to get on with, it is much easier to blame them for being 'difficult' than to look within to discover why you are labelling this interaction thus.

Progress now
Who is 'difficult'?

If you ever use the term 'difficult people', take a moment to think what that means. Think of a person who is 'difficult'. What exactly is it they do or think which makes them difficult for you to deal with?

For example, they may be acting as they do because:

- You find it hard to build rapport with them.
- They mismatch you in a number of ways.
- Their moral stance or value system is at odds with your own.

- ◑ They do not acknowledge you or your ideas.
- ◑ They never seem to be curious or ask questions.
- ◑ They do not want to learn anything new or be better at things.

Now that you have identified some of the triggers for your response, *where* exactly does the 'difficulty' lie? Can you point to its location?

In order to answer this question, you need to look at how you use language and metaphors. The word 'difficult' is a label you apply to some aspect of the world. The 'difficulty' is indicative of your lack of flexibility in dealing with that other person. Of course, you may be fully justified in finding them hard to build rapport with. The other person may have a very different worldview and be unwilling to shift on anything. Recognizing that is one step. Using the Four Realities Model, you can do something about it.

Progress now

A change journey through the perceptual positions

Journeys change people. Metaphorical journeys change how they think, how they code reality, and subsequently, how they behave. Try this little experiment.

1   Think of that 'difficult' person in your life. Make it stronger: someone who really annoys you, drives you crazy! Notice the thoughts and feelings you have when you think of that person or that incident in the past.

2   Now consider: How is it possible to feel this way when this person is not physically present but just in your imagination?

The answer is: relationships do not exist 'out there' in the world, but are mental constructs. We remember that other person, and the associated memories, and this triggers our feelings about them. If you want to change that relationship, work on the way those memories are 'coded' in your mind. You can do this by perceiving this relationship from different points of view. The original thoughts and feelings were from First Position, imagining that relationship.

3 Now clear your mind of those thoughts and feelings by physically moving to change your state.

'Physicalize' the metaphors

Do this exercise by literally moving to a different position on the floor. It becomes easier to see what is going on by physicalizing the metaphor. If you want to change the way you respond to another person, this is what you do.

4 Break the usual pattern and move to Second Position so that you can perceive things from the other person's point of view. Copy their style, adopt their posture, how they stand or sit, and the way they speak when they talk to you. Be that other person, looking at 'you over there', and notice how this feels, and what you are thinking as this 'other' person.

5 Step completely out of this relationship, change your state again.

6 Move completely 'outside' of this relationship. Physically stand back where you can see that imagined relationship somewhere in front of you. Focus on the one that looks like you. And from this Third Position, consider: 'How do I respond emotionally to that me over there?'

There are many possible responses: anger, pity, sympathy, bewilderment, etc. Or you may feel like telling that you to 'Stop messing about. Do something!' You are judging that 'habitual' you according to your values – and with feeling!

7   Step aside into a Fourth Position, from where you can see the other three positions. You are going to 'scramble' the way things are currently organized. A simple way is by exchanging the First Position you with the Third Position you, so that the decisive, judgemental you plays a stronger part in that relationship. No longer will you be the 'passive victim' or whatever you were with that other person. This relationship has now changed!

Fourth Position allows you to indulge in a little creative magic as you 'perturb' the system. You have no idea what will happen, but you know it will be different. Trusting your inbuilt requirement for self-preservation, you may assume the change will be for the better. And as you change, this will have an effect on the other person.

8   Check what has changed by returning to First Position, to be the new you. Notice how it is different now.

9   Then return to Second Position as the other person looking at the revised version of you. This relationship has changed, hasn't it?

10 Finally, return to being yourself in First Position, and begin living this revitalized you.

THE NATURE OF THE PROCESS

The essential nature of the process from First to Fourth Position is shifting from compliance and conformity with 'the way things are' to challenging that 'truth' and taking personal responsibility for having created that particular problem in the first place! By accepting responsibility, you also acknowledge your own capability for creating something better.

Conflict is one result of the way you have coded your experience of that other person. Your relationship belongs to the cognitive realm, which is why it is necessary to change mind-sets, rather than merely change the physical environment or context in which change happens. Although cognitive change does occur when you change the context, it still retains its unpredictability.

If you experience hostility, resistance, indifference, and so on, then having this perceptual flexibility leads to realizing that you are 'part of the problem'. Being stuck in First Position has the potential for conflict whenever you perceive another person as 'not like me' or as an 'enemy'. If your way of being is threatened, you may dig your heels in, resist alternative ideas, or go into denial. You blame others, or treat them as somehow unworthy of the same rights and considerations that you claim. Ultimately you might dismiss them as mad, evil or dangerous, and treat them as sub-human. Each society seems to have its scapegoats and outcasts — applied to anyone who disagrees with the truth held by those in power and who need to control others. Then, moving to Second Position is seen as weakness; you fear the loss of your own personal boundaries.

In Fourth Position you realize that you can create any boundaries you want, that no truths are eternal or fixed. From the higher Level III sense of universal awareness, change flows down and affects cognition on Level II and behaviour on Level I.

It is useful to assume that all human behaviour is purposeful — even though you may not be aware of what that purpose is — and that people want to do their best. By moving to Second Position, you can explore the nature of someone else's rationality and its validity. Although they may appear to you to be behaving irrationally, you find they are perfectly consistent within their own framework of reality. The value and function of being able to 'Second Position' others is that you get to find out 'where they are coming from' and that allows you to gain rapport with them. Then you can begin to lead them to somewhere else.

CHAPTER 9
Conflict

The key to unlocking openness at work is to teach people to give up having to be in agreement. We think agreement is so important. Who cares? You have to bring paradoxes, conflicts, and dilemmas out in the open, so collectively we can be more intelligent than we can be individually.

PETER SENGE

If you see in any given situation only what everybody else can see, you can be said to be so much a representative of your culture that you are a victim of it.

S. I. HAYAKAWA

CREATING CONFLICT

Despite your best-laid plans, change inevitably generates conflict, resistance or tension. There are going to be times when it will be like persuading sweet-toothed children to eat sour apples. You are bound to meet resistance if you have not sold the benefits to them in an appropriate way. Not everyone will believe that something nasty now will be of great benefit to them later. In order that your message may be heard, you need to remove these stumbling blocks on your path to success.

Select any belief and there will surely be someone who contradicts it. Conflict is the yeast that enlivens your interaction with the world. Rather than something to be avoided at all costs, treat conflict as your next challenge for proving your understanding. Be grateful that your 'opponents' are providing this opportunity for personal development. As Walt Whitman inquires:

> Have you learned lessons only of those who admired you, and were tender with you, and stood aside for you? Have you not learned great lessons from those who brace themselves against you, and dispute the passage with you?

When you encounter conflict, or find your options reduced, treat that as a message that the project or the people need your attention. People who wish to avoid upset will resist any changes to the status quo. Those who have a vested interest in your activities – even at several stages removed – may also be stirred into opposition by what they imagine the ramifications of the change may be. Particular disputes may blow over if left alone, but frequently things deteriorate if you ignore what is happening. The sooner you intervene, the better. Being able to identify where people are coming from in terms of the reality mode they are using informs of possible responses. When you engage face-to-face with people who have entrenched positions, you will be better at managing your state (they will no longer be able to push your buttons).

Fortunately you have a lifetime's familiarity with conflict resolution, both through direct experience, and indirectly from stories. All powerful stories and dramas are based on conflict, and demonstrate ways in which disputes can be exacerbated and then settled. From the first interruption of everyday routine until the final showdown, the Hero attempts to restore harmony. What matters is that in the process, the main characters get to understand other points of view, and update their own thinking. Having accepted the new reality, they explore the consequences. By envisaging the whole process, and by seeing things from everyone's point of view, you can reduce potential opposition to your plans. Explain what is likely to happen to everyone involved, and outline the potential benefits for them. Telling an appropriate motivational story improves the probability of the change being welcomed.

Motivating people is a continual challenge. Because desires and frustrations come and go, the solutions will be forever changing, and you must demonstrate flexibility and adaptability. The more you are 'living your vision,' the more you will be able to see things from a variety of points of view. This increases your influence, as you come across as being congruent and authentic. But there are no guarantees. There is no sure way of changing someone's pessimistic attitude to one of optimism. Put yourself in their position to get a sense of 'What's in it for them?' – there must be a perceived benefit of being pessimistic. Before you can move anywhere else with them, you should honour that benefit, and ensure that if it is so vital to them, they can get it another way.

RESPONSE TO CONFLICT

Here are four possible responses to conflict.

- ₪ **Fight.** The Fighter's response is to dig in and fight their corner.

- ₪ **Flight.** In the interests of self-preservation, the Flyer chooses to be somewhere else. In the wisdom of Schulz's *Peanuts* strip cartoon: 'There is no problem so great that you cannot run away from it.' Failing this, they give in to demands, avoid upset at all costs; keep the peace by placating.

- ₪ **Freeze.** The Freezer delays their response. They stay cool, calm and collected. They analyse what is happening, buying time to consider their next move. Doing nothing is a way of being invisible.

- ₪ **Flow.** The Free-spirit goes with the flow. They establish exquisite rapport with the aggressor, and defuse the expected conflict by accepting their opponent's truth by agreeing with them: 'You're absolutely right!' They are teaching them to play a new game. Here are Bogart (Marlowe) and Bacall (Rutlidge) in Howard Hawks' (1948) movie, *The Big Sleep*:

Rutlidge: I don't like your manners.

Marlowe: I don't mind if you don't like my manners. I don't like them myself. They're pretty bad. I grieve over them long winter evenings.

WHERE ARE PEOPLE COMING FROM?

Resolving a dispute is easier if you can recognize the nature of the disagreement. The Four Realities model describes a number of basic conflict patterns, and offers ways towards resolution. However, you still need to develop rapport and find practical ways of intervening in specific contexts.

It is easy to mismatch other people's worldviews because every person has a unique interpretation of their own life experience. When you misunderstand their communication, you may describe the other person as 'off the wall' or 'from another planet'. But instead of being dismissive, or trying to smooth over the cracks, pay attention to how such conflict is occurring. Stand back and seek underlying patterns. Be curious about their worldview, and elicit information about their beliefs, preferences and expectations; discover what matters to them, the patterns of their thinking.

There could be clues to which worldview you are up against, in how you describe the other person who is 'not on your wavelength'. Which of the following derogatory terms might you use for people you don't along with?

Table 9.1 'Difficult' types

Type name	Possible mode
Fundamentalist, Jobsworth, Dictator, Bully, Hothead, In-your-face.	Unitary
Scientific, Propeller-head, Nerd, Egg-head, Boffin, Professor, Cold Fish.	Sensory
Emotional, Sensitive, Touchy-feely, People-person, Security blanket.	Social
Artistic, Creative, Head-in-the-clouds, Ideas-person, Visionary, Off with the fairies.	Mythic

How you label someone else depends upon where you are coming from. And just as you find certain other people difficult to get on with, they in turn may find you peculiar, weird, or an oddball. The degree of matching of the different worldviews affects the extent to which people like, get on with or understand one another. Having recognized where someone else is coming from, you can then choose to be more like them, or choose to be more different. And you could be a role model of acceptance by cultivating your Level III spiritual understanding and thus demonstrate that it is possible to rise above all that.

DEALING WITH UNITARY TYPES

Strong Unitary types (people with a fixed worldview) can be hard to budge, as they resist other points of view. They are secure when bound by their well-defined rules and obligations. They believe their version of reality is 'the truth'; their way of doing things the 'correct' way. Tell them your version and they just 'don't get it'. Unitary thinking is resistant to:

- **Sensory.** Rational debate because that pluralistic reality offers choice and therefore doubt. 'People can justify what they do in all kinds of ways, by twisting logic . . .'.

- **Social.** Personal judgements violate the impersonal, given rules. Group needs are based on feelings and desires, which are not to be trusted. 'Just because a number of people behave like that does not make it right.'

- **Mythic.** Personal choice, freewill. 'What would happen if everyone just did as they liked?'

Actually, you know this place, because of the feeling of stability and predictability you get by languaging and storying the world. Sometimes you need this certainty; at times of change you must let go, so that learning may happen.

When working with others, having an overview of all points of view gives you the advantage, but you must tread carefully if you are going to maintain rapport, and help them adjust to a position which is more tolerant of alternative interpretations. Before they will do anything differently, they may need 'permission' from a higher authority. A key word is *obedience*. Given your higher status or authority, in *your* context *you* spell out the rules, provide a framework that matches Unitary preferences for top-down structures and authority patterns. You could insist that 'In this project these are the rules that apply.' Make explicit the operating principles: 'When you are here, this is how you have to behave . . .'.

You could instruct them to enter a special 'project mode' – a Second Position shift – in which they become a 'different person' (see p. 176). For example, they could be allocated a specific role or asked to act in the manner of one of their role models. Actually or metaphorically they could wear a hat or uniform to indicate which role or context they are in. This approach is similar to that suggested by Edward de Bono in his 'Six Thinking Hats' (1991: 5) procedure. He says:

This method may seem extremely simple and even childish — but it does work. It works because it sets the rules of the game, and people then can be asked to play the game. People feel foolish if they don't seem to be able to follow the rules.

In other words, make it safe for people to be different somehow. Depending on the situation, and the strength of resistance you encounter, you could:

- Ask them to leave. This is an appropriate strategy if you have the power to decide who may join the project. Unwilling 'conscripts' are likely to be disruptive and spoil the experience for others.

- Assume that they have two other reality modes functioning reasonably well, and that when encouraged they will shift to them. This means finding out their next preferred mode.

- Use some linguistic strategies for shifting them: 'Has this always been true?', 'What would be the most important thing for you to do right now?'

CHUNKING UP TO FIND AGREEMENT

Because people get bogged down in detail, it is good idea to have them metaphorically stand back and notice the bigger picture. Once they 'disengage' they can get a more objective overview of the issue, and shift their thinking from the particular to the general. Considering a conflict in terms of its principles and ultimate aims is likely to shed light on what they really want to achieve. For instance, if someone wants to prevent your change project from happening, it could be because they want to preserve their job, or because they are concerned about having to learn new systems.

Help put things into perspective, by suggesting:

- 'So what would that look like from back here, from the outside, as it were?' and have them physically step back far enough to see the whole context.

- 'Imagine you are standing in a cinema projection room, knowing that there are any number of movies that you could be projecting on the screen . . .'.

- 'It's like being up in the circle of a theatre, looking down at the illuminated stage, and realizing that all kinds of dramas could be played out down there . . .'

SHIFTING TO NEUTRAL

The Four Realities Model indicates possible conflict whenever two single modes polarize and vie for dominance. You can move towards agreement by having both parties move to the same mode. If it is one preferred by one side, that could give them the advantage. Moving both parties to neutral territory, such as a less-preferred mode for both of them, allows them to both then explore the nature of their disagreement, and thus gain understanding. For example, if a creative type (Mythic) and an analytical type (Sensory) get into an argument, if both move to Social mode you can have them explore their values and priorities for what needs to happen. Because people all use all four modes in their thinking, it should usually be possible to find some common ground. Making an effort to think in a non-preferred way becomes easier with practice.

THREE MAJOR CONFLICTS

However, with some combinations of thinking styles it is not possible to find neutral territory and therefore it is difficult to get people to shift at all. There are three combinations of two reality modes (Table 9.2) which generate conflict (McWhinney, 1995).

Table 9.2 Three major conflicts

Sacred (Unitary + Mythic)	vs	Secular (Sensory + Social)
Scientific (Unitary + Sensory)	vs	Humanistic (Social + Mythic)
Normative (Unitary + Social)	vs	Creative (Sensory + Mythic)

These polarized ways of perceiving the world are widespread. As neither side has anything in common with the other side, and with no neutral territory to move to, these kinds of conflict tend to perpetuate themselves, and would appear to be generally unresolvable at this level. Historically, we know that many sectarian conflicts seem inextinguishable. Despite gains and losses on both sides, years pass and still the conflict continues, lasting for decades or even centuries, with little result. Some feuds are only worked out when the members of one side eventually die out. Even in scientific circles acceptance can be slow. For example, Galileo's notion of planetary motion has only recently been accepted by the Vatican. The debate remains confused because people are arguing from different reality modes, and the underlying structure of the conflict is never clarified. Therefore it would be useful to cover briefly how such 'eternal' conflicts arise. Although peace is a worthy aim, conventional dispute-solving techniques seem unable to achieve it because resolution is not available at the same level as the conflict. Continuing to use processes which fail to produce results wastes time and resources. Finding solutions begins by understanding how conflict arises from the very way we perceive reality.

FREEWILL VS DETERMINISM

'I don't know if we each have a destiny, or if we're all just floating around, accidental like, on a breeze. But I think . . . Maybe it's both. Maybe both are happening at the same time.'
FORREST (TOM HANKS) IN *FORREST GUMP*, 1997

The first major conflict is between the belief that the universe is determined for you, contrasted with the belief that you have freewill to do what you want. This is one of the basic dimensions of the four realities grid. Remember that there is no 'right answer' here; you need both kinds of belief to understand experience.

McWhinney suggests that it might be better to call these conflicts 'stand-offs' as there are no direct approaches for resolving the conflict. When the Sacred (Unitary + Mythic) comes up against the Secular (Sensory + Social), avoidance or enforced separation become the way of living. The alternative is a war to the death, so that one side 'wins'.

NATURE VS NURTURE

The second major conflict is between the Scientific (Unitary + Sensory) and the Humanistic (Social + Mythic), and manifests in the scientific community as the ongoing nature vs nurture debate on how you get to be the way you are. Which is more important: genetic inheritance – what you start out with; or social upbringing – what you learn? In other words: 'Is what happens determined externally by some unknown external power, or do I have control over my own actions?'

Thinking in this polarized way misses the point that we use all perceptual positions and reality modes to understand our humanity. They all exist simultaneously, and we dip in and out of them all at various times. The more important question is: which way of thinking is most appropriate for *this* issue, *this* piece of action, learning or understanding?

We need both the technological benefits of science and the humanistic benefits of society so that our lives and work may be fulfilling. Gradually the two communities find ways of coming together, as is happening with traditional medicine and complementary health practices.

ARTISTIC VS MORALISTIC

The third dichotomy involves the contrast between the creative Artist (Mythic + Sensory) and the normative Moralist (Unitary + Social). By combining the modes on the diagonals we have the types which McWhinney labels Normative (U + So) and Creative (M + Se).

The artistic explorer always want to expand the realms of human knowledge; the moralists are more concerned with limiting freedom, defining what is appropriate and establishing the norms of acceptable behaviour.

Artistic types are for ever deriding the Moralists, and this manifests in our society in parody, cartoons, and TV programmes that satirize those who desire to control. Politicians are often worried about the freedom of the media, and may impose censorship if they have the power to do so. Such behaviour can be identified over hundreds of years in different cultures; it would appear that not much changes. Times of restriction alternate with times of freedom of expression: each accepts the other as a thorn in the flesh; each provides material for the other to complain about.

THE *COMET* STORY

The world's first passenger jet airliner – the *Comet* – was put into service in 1952. Yet within two years, after four major accidents which killed more than 100 people, the whole *Comet* fleet was grounded. This failure was partly a result of the conflicting interests of those who wanted this project to succeed. Essentially there was a conflict between the values involved (social reality) and the technological design (sensory reality).

Social values are often built around status, and to governments being first becomes a priority. In this story, the pressures were as follows:

🔊 **Commercial**. To get British jet aircraft into service ahead of the Americans/competition. Britain wanted to be first and to reap the rewards. (However, America was further behind than they thought.)

🔊 **Economic**. To set up a million pound industry for the future. In austerity-bound, post-war Britain, the Labour government was urging manufacturers to 'export or die'. The *Comet* offered the hope of millions of pounds of desperately needed export orders.

- 🔖 **Political**. To meet the government's launch date. The belief that America would soon adopt jet aircraft technology and overtake them if there were any delays.

- 🔖 **Self-esteem**. To maintain/build on the success of innovation and rapid production of wartime aircraft.

- 🔖 **Loyalty**. The manufacturers chose to use their own company engines, despite the fact that they were not powerful enough; Rolls Royce engines would have been better.

In this case, those values overrode the needs of the manufacturing technology. Developing an innovative system takes time, and the period for testing the design in practice was insufficient.

- 🔖 **Materials**. In order to reduce the weight, the *Comet* was clad with a very thin aluminium alloy, which was glued to the airframe. This cladding was unsuitable for high altitude pressure.

- 🔖 **Manufacture**. Because of difficulties in bonding the windows, the construction workers used rivets instead. These created weak points from which the metal skin began to tear under stress.

○ **Time**. Because of the imposed deadlines, the *Comet* was put into service before thoroughly testing the components and stress-testing the aircraft for metal fatigue, despite warnings from the Royal Aircraft Establishment in Farnborough.

○ **Design**. The plane was underpowered, and weight saving had to be made in every area. Instead of using a rival company's more powerful engines, the design was changed to allow for underpowered engines.

In other words, commercial and political pressures took precedence over safety and good design. Unitary thinking was provided – the Royal Aircraft Establishment's guidelines, and testing specifications – but ignored. Creative Mythic thinking got the project into the air, but it also needs to include scenario planning (see p. 000), exploring the likely consequences of decisions made during the manufacturing process.

CONFLICT OVERVIEW

Your aim is not to eliminate conflict, but to accept it as a vital part of learning. If there were no conflict you would be bored! Conflict challenges any fixed ideas, and keeps minds active. If your values are being violated and you are having an emotional response, this may indicate an unresolved issue that could divert your attention from the job in hand.

The Four Realities Model enables you to recognize the platform from which someone is putting their case. Because this way of thinking is uncommon, you may have to educate people so that they gain a greater understanding of conflict, and increase their tolerance of alternative points of view. When people are expressing conflicting views, either look for common ground, or analyse the issues from each Reality mode in turn. If there is no common ground on the Cognitive level, raise people to Level III/Spirit/Fifth Position. Agreement can often be reached by eliciting the highest principles which are honoured by all concerned. In Fifth Position, people are 'above the conflict' and boundaries between people tend to dissolve. From here they are able to perceive that all beliefs about the world are 'figments of the imagination' which have their place in the more limited middle domain of Mind.

FINDING SOLUTIONS

The Perceptual Positions Model offers a way of exploring conflicts. Gather answers to: 'How would each position view this?' and seek the major sticking points. You know that for any view there will be those who will either not understand other views (because they do not match their way of thinking) or will reject them out of hand (because they violate their value system). Given their attitude, make an informed guess at where they are coming from, and then find a way of reframing their understanding, by shifting their position and broadening their outlook.

A fundamental difference in how people want to solve problems will make an early appearance: *Convergent [Unitary + Social] thinking* – wanting to maintain control, restrict behaviour, reduce options, apply legal sanctions; and *Divergent [Sensory + Mythic] thinking* – wanting to creatively open things up, devise innovative, counterintuitive solutions.

You have to decide what exactly the problem is that you want to solve. Once you have decided which issue to address, use the different modes of thinking and consider the insights they might offer.

FIFTH POSITION THINKING

Fifth Position offers an overview of the impasse on Level II. You can metaphorically observe the drama from a vantage point high up in a theatre. If you were the director of the play that is unfolding in front of you, how would you intervene and direct the characters? Notice their habits and limiting patterns of action, and devise ways of interrupting them. What new element could you introduce that would upset the 'unthinking' behaviour? Doing anything different will change the dynamics. Each step brings a fresh point of view, and people will be thinking differently in some respect.

Think beyond the impasse by asking: 'In time, could this be healed?' If Yes: 'How would that happen?' Get them to apply their wisdom to solve it. After all, they have a lot more experience of running this pattern than you do. If No: 'Do you want to go on being a victim, or do you want to take more control over your life?' (Of course, they may want to go on believing that they do not have the power to do this.)

LEARNING FROM CONFLICT

Assessing and resolving conflicts contribute to the growth of wisdom. You learn how people perceive their realities, and devise ways of intervening in order to create appropriate changes and restore balance. As a change manager, your task is to explore multiple points of view, and to take global, ecological factors into account. Change does not happen in isolation. You need to consider how far a particular issue reaches, both sideways into the social community, and forwards in time.

Treat conflict as a message from the universe that someone's thinking is becoming rigid or limited. Having a limited vision leads to simplistic solutions which will eventually fail. Because all solutions fail at some time, it is better to see any particular solution as the basis for sorting out the next set of problems. And because any intervention will have some far-reaching consequences, stretch your imagination by developing some scenarios that will enable you to follow through each intervention as far as possible into the future. But first you need to find out the extent to which the world has already shifted, by noticing the feedback you are getting.

CHAPTER 10
Reflective Practice

Reflection is not just thoughtful practice but a learning experience.

JARVIS, QUOTED IN BURNS AND BULMAN, 2000: 173

To doubt everything or to believe everything are two equally convenient solutions; both dispense with the necessity of reflection.

JULES HENRI POINCARÉ

WHAT HAPPENED?

When a change project finishes, the ties are cut and the team disbands. The challenges have been met, the conflicts resolved, and the project has now been completed. For you it may seem a satisfying release as you move onto your next project. For those who have been benefitting from your interventions, this is the beginning of the next stage of their journey in which they will learn to manage the changes that have been wrought. Will this 'learning experience' continue to help them as they move into their future?

Was the vision fulfilled, the original situation ' transformed' into one that everyone is pleased with? Now is the time to take time for debriefing all those who have been involved and for making a formal assessment of what actually happened. If you just assume or pretend that everything worked well, and ignore the reality, you miss the opportunity of learning from what worked and what didn't. If, when the project finishes, you immediately rush on to the next one, you may never get to find out 'What happens next?' You also lose out if you cannot remember exactly what you did (through poor record keeping), and then cannot relate your plans and actions to what actually happened. In the hurly-burly of a project it is easy to forget the details – especially the 'good' things. By keeping a detailed log of significant events, with your comments on them, you are setting up triggers for recalling memorable experiences for later analysis. Therefore, make later recall easier by jotting down some notes at the time, while the events are still fresh in your mind.

Nothing ever works out exactly as planned. Even though you were expecting the unexpected, you still had to think on your feet, making sense of those unforeseen events that did not fit your preconceived ideas. Make it OK for people to talk about the 'deviations from the plan' because it is from the 'mistakes' that you learn the most.

There is a strange consequence that sometimes arises when setting a goal. Expectations are raised; the gap between where you are now and where you want to be increases; and this gives the illusion that things are getting *worse* because you interpret the bigger gap as meaning you are dropping behind. The reality is that you are improving, only now you have a more distant goal.

WHAT DO YOU PAY ATTENTION TO?

People frequently misinterpret what happens. No event can be described in its totality because every view is partial, every person biased by their own beliefs. People tend to pay attention to what appears most salient, has highest value for them, provides relevant information – about themselves, other people, and their context. One form of bias is the 'availability error'. Perception is affected by what first comes to mind, or by anything that has made a deep impression. The psychologist Stuart Sutherland (1992: 21) adds that: '. . . Recently presented material is available, but it has also been found that anything that produces strong emotion, that is dramatic, that leads to the formation of images and that is concrete rather than abstract is also readily available.'

People also invent explanations based on:

> **False reasoning.** Poorly conducted surveys may unwittingly include bias. The psychiatrist Johann Hari (2002) comments that 'In over 100 years' worth of case studies I've looked at, I have never seen a single case of incest that has ended happily.' He admits that by their very nature psychiatrists do not attract happy, functional people.

🖰 **Superstition.** A belief that something must always be present because you link it with times when things worked well. The downside is the debilitating belief that if you lose your lucky rabbit-paw or forget your ritual incantation, then some terrible doom awaits you.

🖰 **Mind-reading.** Guessing that you know how other people are thinking, feeling or will respond to events: 'I know exactly how you feel.' No, you don't!

🖰 **Denial.** Being unwilling to accept what is happening, even in the face of the evidence: 'This can't be true. These kinds of things don't happen to us.'

🖰 **Political expediency.** Placing a high value on what others will think about you: 'This would do us no favours if it were splashed in the newspapers.'

🖰 **False objectivity.** To what extent are *you* part of the problem? Although you may think you are a 'neutral' observer, you are not, because you are part of the system. Even when 'doing nothing', or 'just watching', you are exerting some influence over others.

🖰 **Naive innocence.** Arguments and disputes are never one-sided: 'It takes two to tango'. Take responsibility for what happened by considering 'In what way am *I* exquisitely creating this difficulty, tension, or impasse?' or 'What are *we* are doing that creates that particular response from the other people?'

REFLECTING ON WHAT HAPPENED

> We learn best from experience, but we never directly experience the consequences of many of our most important decisions.
>
> PETER SENGE, 1990: 23

Formally reflecting on experience has become a more common practice in recent years. Perhaps the most challenging aspect is setting aside the time to do it. You may delight in recounting disasters and conflicts to your mates down the pub or to friends over a coffee, but be less willing to evaluate your experiences formally. Learning does not happen by stuffing bulging folders into a filing cabinet, or storing documents on a hard-disk.

Reflective practice is more than just thinking about what happened. Consider the challenge that Dorothy faces in the Land of Oz. She has to come to understand the topsy-turvy nature of that world, learn its rules, engage with its inhabitants, so that she can function as part of that society. Eventually, however, as in the best stories, she completes her quest, having helped others, and returns to her own world, enriched by the learning she has acquired along the way.

The model or theoretical frame provides an 'availability bonus' in that it enables you to interpret what happened in meaningful ways, allows you to test your theories, and gain greater understanding. For example, the Four Realities Model offers a way of checking where someone seems to be coming from, and of extending your ability to explore other manifestations of the principles.

Progress now

Comparisons

Reflecting on a project means 'reliving' the narrative of what happened and noticing connections, patterns and regularities. Compare the original state of affairs with the revised state that was achieved by the end of the project, and notice what is different. Imagine seeing those two pictures side by side on a mental screen, and then compare and contrast the 'before' and 'after' versions. Apart from the specific details that you can see, consider the following:

Expectations

🖎 In what specific ways has the original vision been fulfilled?

- ↻ What did you expect to happen? Did you get the changes you wanted – or thought you wanted?
- ↻ What was unexpected, surprising or gave cause for concern?

Processes

- ↻ How effective were the procedures you used?
- ↻ How relevant, appropriate and valid were the models and theories you based your thinking on? What worked? What didn't work? Should you revise these models?

Relationships

- ↻ How have the relationships between the people directly concerned, and between that group and their 'customers' evolved?

Overall success

Estimate the success of this project:

- ↻ How do you know that change has been successful? What is your evidence?
- ↻ How accurate were your targets?
- ↻ What are the key factors of your success?
- ↻ How would you explain what happened?
- ↻ What would you do differently next time?

KEY EVENTS

'Is there any point to which you would wish to draw my attention?'
'To the curious incident of the dog in the night-time.'
'The dog did nothing in the night-time.'
'That was the curious incident,' remarked Sherlock Holmes.

ARTHUR CONAN DOYLE, *THE MEMOIRS OF SHERLOCK HOLMES: SILVER BLAZE*

Key events are those which significantly influence how you think and behave. They are 'turning points' or 'milestones' in your learning, or evidence of 'Oh, right!' You recall a memory and realize 'It was at that moment that things fell into place!' It just happened, out of nowhere. Maybe you were bogged down in a problem and stopped thinking about it. Suddenly someone told you about some incident; or you picked up a book and a sentence caught your eye; or an item on the news got you thinking – and the connection was made, a new meaning emerged.

The good thing about such events – even though they may have seemed challenging or difficult at the time – is that they were indeed life-changing. Now they are able to goad you into further exploration, promise you greater understanding – which is why it is worth identifying these key events as potential resources. They will not necessarily be big and dramatic; they might be 'trivial', even 'throw-away' remarks, or the look in someone's eyes that gives you pause for thought: 'What was *that* about?' The significance of an event only becomes clear in the fullness of time.

DECISIONS

By keeping contemporary records of how you decide what to do, you will be able to see how valid your reasoning was later on. Decision making is not completely rational, because it is unlikely that you will have complete information. Eventually there comes a point when you must stop thinking about the evidence and the logic, and commit to one course of action.

Needing to be 'right', protesting that 'I had to do that. It was the only option available!' may be true, but could demonstrate a lack of imagination. There are always alternatives – although some may appear unrealistic or unobtainable.

Progress now

Critical decisions

Projects do not run from start to finish without adjustments:

- 🍃 Where did you deviate from the plan?
- 🍃 Were the reasons for deviating:
    - 🍃 External? World events changed the rationale for the project.
    - 🍃 Internal? You rethought your intentions and procedures, and realized there was a better way of achieving them.

Consider the major choice points you encountered:

- 🍃 What decisions did you have to make?
- 🍃 At that time, what clear options were there?
- 🍃 How did you decide what to do? What influenced you? What were the important factors?
- 🍃 Was there any point at which you might have terminated the project (for whatever reason) and didn't? What criteria were you considering?

Having made a decision:

- 🍃 What did you expect to happen?
- 🍃 What presuppositions did you make?

WHAT ELSE COULD YOU HAVE DONE?

If you are the kind of person who thrives on regret, looking back at past decisions and thinking: 'If only I'd . . .', then you could stay stuck for a long, long time. Better to make a short visit, learn whatever you need to learn, and then move on. For example, look back at a major decision point and, in the light of what you now know, consider any alternatives that occur to you. Follow each alternative forward into its future to see what is likely to happen. This could inform you about what to do should a similar situation arise in future.

EVALUATION

Social reality is concerned with feelings, values, and judgements. Making superficial evaluations is easy. Using words such as 'rubbish', 'nonsense', 'cool', or 'great' suggests either an emotional attitude, or sloppy thinking about something you cannot be bothered with. A proper evaluation requires further elaboration. If someone uses such glib words, you can choose to enquire into what they mean for that person. Treat the word as standing for a whole conglomeration of feelings and emotions, and ask them to expand and provide evidence: 'In what way is this "nonsense"?' 'What leads you to suggest it is a "great" decision?'

When giving feedback to someone, it is more effective to tell them what they could do better in future. People tend to put themselves and others down unnecessarily, inadvertently using many negative or limiting words such as 'problem', 'difficult', 'weakness', and so on. How about changing your thoughts by talking about 'challenges' or 'something that needs more working on'? Thinking positively may feel strange at first – all new patterns of behaviour require getting used to. Although it may start as slightly jokey, it soon moves on to become your natural way of communicating.

RUSHING TO JUDGEMENT

Making judgements is second nature. Giving 'criticism' usually has a negative slant – you are looking for who is to blame, what did not work, why you did not like it or why you could not make sense of it. The kinds of value words people use may relate to their preferred reality mode. For example:

- **Unitary.** Good/Bad, Correct, Appropriate. (Was this in line with our principles?)

- **Sensory.** Effective, On track, Necessary, Logical. (Did this situation achieve its purpose?)

- **Social.** Important, Valuable, For the best. (What matters about what happened?)

- **Mythic.** Interesting, Stimulating, Creative. (What further opportunities did this open up?)

Progress now

Personal change

Exploring change has to affect you personally, and it is valuable to appreciate your own growth in understanding. Consider:

- ▷ 'What was the most valuable thing to come out of this change process?'
- ▷ 'What have I learned from this?'
- ▷ 'How has this project affected my understanding of the business I am in?'
- ▷ 'Have there been any significant shifts to your understanding of other people?'

In the light of what you have learned from your change project, is your 'working theory' good enough or do you need to develop a better, more useful model or paradigm?

REFLECTING

The final piece of reflective practice is to do nothing. Simply let everything you have been thinking about settle. Switch off conscious thought and allow your mind to do what it does best – assimilate the information. To coin a phrase, 'Learning happens'. All you have to do is get out of the way. You can set up the conditions that promote learning and be open to what emerges.

One way of testing your understanding is to tell someone else what you have learned. Doing this is good practice for finding the essence of the learning. You will probably have to give a report to various people who have an interest in what happened. Your report provides evidence that the project has been worthwhile. Different audiences will require this information in different ways. The story you tell them, based on the key points, will allow them to share the acquired wisdom. This account should also inspire the people in the organization to move forward with more realistic expectations, clearer outcomes and more relevant visions. This is how they can update their own models of change; they will be able to adopt best practice for acting or intervening in the future.

Progress now

Brief stories

To get to the essence, and for practising being succinct, try telling the story of what happened in less than one minute. Use this format:

- ✎ Explain the context – where and when this took place.

- ✎ Say why you did it: 'In order to change the way . . .' or whatever.

- ✎ Briefly describe the events. What happened? Instead of rambling, you are going to be explicit and get straight to the essence: 'And the point of this is . . .'

- ✎ Your audience will want to know what is in it for them, so make this clear as well: 'The benefit of this for you is . . .' This means you have thought about it from their point of view.

This way of telling the story focuses your mind, and forces you to eliminate irrelevancies. Make everything you say count. Because it is clearly designed for others to understand, they will listen to you, knowing that it will be a worthwhile experience for them.

TRANSFERABILITY

Keep the energy going by looking to the future. How can your conclusions be applied to new situations, to other contexts? Is your current best practice something that will prove useful in the future?

- If not, what needs to be changed or tweaked?
- Can this be generalized to other contexts/situations?
- If you were to apply this in other contexts (specifically: . . .) what would probably happen?

In the light of what you have learned from this project, consider:

- 'Where else could I use this information?'
- 'How would this work with such-and-such group of people?'
- 'What would be different if we changed the sequence, speed, perceptual position, and so on?'

Essentially this comes down to: 'If you had to do it again, what would you do differently?' 'How would you change what you used to do as a consequence of what you have learned?' And 'What would be the implications if you were to do that?'

SETTING A FRAME FOR LEARNING

Part of your role as project leader is to help other people understand the changes that happen. You *Inform* them of what to pay attention to, and suggest criteria for categorizing experience by setting a frame, explaining the context, and indicating the kinds of change that will be taking place. Then they will be able to integrate the new information into their own lives in ways which make sense to them.

You help them *Reform* their understanding by having people perceive events from several points of view, and by thinking about what has changed in an abstract or theoretical way. They contemplate possible consequences, likely problems, and so on, in their imagination.

An essential part of reflective learning is to consider what actually happened in relation to what you expected or wanted to happen. In other words, you assess the power of your imagination by exploring 'what happens next' in a number of stories or scenarios.

Emerging from reflection, the *Transformative* stage of learning is the most significant. You are making the learning your own. This happens when you engage wholeheartedly with the world that you have created through your actions, so that you get to know its ramifications, make new connections, develop a relationship with it, and get a sense of ownership.

Ownership means acceptance: this is how things are right now; these are the resources I have for continuing to work with change. Accepting the fluidity of life allows you to be more open and to be part of the flow of experience that leads to greater understanding.

CHAPTER 11
What Happens Next?

Certainly the pace of science and technology continues to accelerate. [. . .] The number of people engaged in the enterprise of inventing new things has just exploded. The rewards of new invention are so great that what we are seeing is a dramatic proliferation of really radical new technologies . . .

PETER SCHWARTZ, PRESIDENT OF GLOBAL BUSINESS NETWORK

The only way to discover the limits of the possible is to go beyond them, to the impossible.

ARTHUR C. CLARKE, *PROFILES OF THE FUTURE*, 1962

LOOKING FORWARD

Change starts with changing minds: how you perceive your reality. The Perceptual Positions Model offers six fundamentally different ways of interpreting experience. When you consider a range of points of view it becomes obvious that problems and issues are more complex than you once thought. You also realize that simple solutions often lead to confusion, and you will need to backtrack. Acknowledging that every view is valid in its own terms, and that all views are 'best attempts so far' (and that ideals are unattainable) you can explore issues with others rather than simply imposing your ideas on them. Working together you will develop good enough strategies for deciding what to do to realize your vision.

Now it is time to look forward to how you can use what you have learned in contexts which matter to you. If your current practice is not helping you achieve all that you want, or if you are not learning as much as you might, then release your grip on what you have been taking as 'fixed', reflect on your experience, and rewrite your stories so that they work for you. The more you are able to acknowledge your biases, move beyond your old way of thinking, the greater will be your impact; you will be acting as a role model for others.

Progress now

Personal change

Take a moment to consider how your thinking has changed as a result of reading this book, doing the 'Progress now' exercises, applying the ideas, and above all, learning to perceive the world in a different way. Having encountered the ideas in this book:

- ⟳ What have you learned about yourself?
- ⟳ How are you thinking differently?
- ⟳ What can you 'see' now that was invisible before?
- ⟳ What are you doing differently?
- ⟳ How have your relationships with other people been changing?
- ⟳ How will you be applying these ideas in the future?

CHALLENGING THE STATUS QUO

> You see things and you say 'Why?'
> But I dream things that never were; and I say 'Why not?'
>
> GEORGE BERNARD SHAW, *BACK TO METHUSELAH*, ACT I

Questioning 'Why do we do this in this way?' can lead to innovative solutions, and competitive advantage. Edward de Bono's 'lateral thinking' concept is based on such 'What if . . . ?' thinking. For example: why pay extra for overseas phone-calls? What if customers just paid for access to the telephone system? We access the internet this way, and even pay a fixed monthly fee for unlimited time. Some restaurants have a set charge, an entry fee, and you eat as much as you want. How could you apply this concept to your business?

Finding opportunities

How can you meet new needs, exploit gluts or surpluses, or find new uses for obsolete products? These are opportunities for being even better at what you do, for enhancing your resources, building on current practice, adding value to existing products and processes, using your creativity to invent new concepts by connecting disparate ideas, finding further applications for old principles, in different contexts.

ANALOGIES AND METAPHORS

Learning happens by making connections, linking new experiences to what you already know. You can be deliberately creative by juxtaposing disparate ideas, or using a 'random' word as a stimulus, and then allowing your mind to create associations and explore the implications of this new arrangement. For example, how could you link up: *Computing* with *Bottles*; *The Future* with *Bakery*; *Transformation* with *Plastic*?

HUMOUR

Much humour results from reframing: suddenly seeing some event from two points of view simultaneously produces an explosion of laughter, and what seemed to be fixed loses its rigidity. People learn better when they are having fun, as they are more open to alternatives. It was a tradition in the Shao Lin temple in China for students, at the end of their course, to deliberately send up their teaching, to poke fun at the seriousness of their studies. Could you find a way of incorporating this into your way of working?

EXPANDING THE FRAME

People often make decisions based on 'gut feeling' rather than logic. They do whatever it takes as long as it feels right, fair, just or moral. There is no way of assessing whether such decisions are 'correct'. Your interpretation can only be based on your limited understanding of the wider system in which they operate. People do not always make their values and feelings public until it comes to the crunch. The further you explore the greater context of any issue, the more you will meet an expanding system of views, value systems, moralities, notions of fairness, justice, third world issues, minority rights, and so forth. If this is a difficult area to consider, there are plenty of people and organizations around who can help you!

MAINTAINING CHANGE

The sad fact is that most change fades away, often very quickly, if it is not nurtured and maintained well. When you have assisted other people to make changes in their lives, the best thing you can do is to provide ongoing support, mentoring. It is hard living the new way, and easy to become disheartened and slip back into old patterns. If you have someone you can call on, to discuss your feelings, and progress, it becomes easier to maintain your own progress and ongoing change.

WHAT HAPPENS NEXT?

> Louis, I think this is the beginning of a beautiful friendship.
>
> CLOSING LINE OF *CASABLANCA*, 1942

Rick (Humphrey Bogart) delivers that classic line to Renault (Claude Rains) as they stride out across the airfield, into the night and the unknown future. Stories often end with the hero riding off into the sunset, or with church bells ringing. But what happens next? Will that relationship work? Do people live happily ever after?

Stories have boundaries – beginnings and endings – which are 'arbitrary', but convenient because they assist understanding. Stories encompass 'complete' events in which most of the issues are resolved and the story feels 'finished'. But real life is not a story. Storying our experiences reduces our ability to think outside that frame. It is a challenge to imagine a story that is beyond the known reality. For instance, in 1876, Sir William Preece, chief engineer of the British Post Office, claimed that 'The Americans have need of the telephone, but we do not. We have plenty of messenger boys.'

The advent of personal computing met with a subdued response when, in 1980, IBM boasted that they had calculated that the world market for personal computers in the coming decade would be 275,000. In 2002, there were 26 million PCs in the UK alone. On the other hand, portable computers plus mobile phones were envisaged in the 1970s by Nicholas Negroponte, who imagined 'a watch that knows who you are, and, as you walk around, your user interface to this ubiquitous network follows you.' Another prediction was the 'Negroponte Implosion' – where show business, publishing and computing coalesced. However, the paperless office now seems laughable; we are inundated with faxes, photocopies, everything duplicated, despite the fact that everything can be digitized and stored on disk. Ink on paper is still the reading medium of choice.

When a need for closure or achieving an outcome dominates your thinking, the future gets forgotten. Further goals, targets and visions must all wait. It is like having a vast billboard filling your view so that you see nothing besides or beyond. You have only reached the end of one particular episode. To find out what happens next, continue the journey, keep the story running. Every time you are tempted to complete, ask 'What happens next?'

SCENARIOS

Scenario-writing is a structured technique for envisioning possible futures by applying narrative structure to specific issues relating to your business. Prepare for the future when you have time to think flexibly, rather than when things are already going wrong and you are paralysed by fear or firefighting a disaster.

When creating scenarios, consider at least three alternatives. Apart from best-case and worst-case projections, include those that get you thinking laterally, or 'thinking the unthinkable'. If instead of thinking, 'That would never happen to us!' you plan for potential disasters ahead of time, you will be ready for what happens. Increase the richness of your scenarios by exploring possible consequences from a variety of points of view. Peter Schwartz (1991: 200) says that:

> Using scenarios is rehearsing the future. You run through the simulated events as if you were already living them. You train yourself to recognise which drama is unfolding. That helps you avoid unpleasant surprises, and know how to act.

He goes on to warn that:

> Unfortunately, reality does not follow even the best-thought-out scenario. The point of scenario-planning is to help us suspend our disbelief in all the futures: to allow us to think that any one of them might take place. Then we can prepare for what we don't think is going to happen.

SCHWARTZ, 1991: 203

Thinking through your range of scenarios sets a frame in your mind that primes you to notice what actually happens. You can notice how and when events deviate from the script, and use those opportunities advantageously. Using scenarios may put you ahead of the game, but you still need practice in noticing trends and spotting clues about ideas that will take off.

MOVEMENT

Stories involve movement, and show people changing how they think, act and relate to others. Sometimes people move along a single dimension and deal with a polarity and achieve balance by incorporating it. For example, moving from *being afraid* to *being self-confident*; moving from *focusing on minute details* to *getting the big picture*. A trio of simple scenarios exemplify resolving the three major conflicts:

- Moving from feeling controlled by events to taking full responsibility for one's own life.

- Moving from thinking there is only one way of doing things to realizing that there is choice.

- Having created a number of options, deciding which particular plan to implement.

Further scenarios involve moving around all four reality modes, completing the loop, as it were. Each change moves the person or project across a threshold. Individuals gradually transform themselves; organizations, societies, ideas, projects, businesses and economies advance and evolve.

261

Overall trends are visible in Western society. For example, over the last few decades there has been a gradual movement from Social reality (the group, society) to Mythic reality (the individual). Social cohesion diminishes as people prefer to do their own thing. Professor Robert Putnam (2000) noticed that whereas people used to go bowling after work, this pastime has greatly diminished in American society. Many prefer to surf the net on their PCs rather than engage in social activities. Meal times are solitary affairs; families eating together around the table is increasingly rare. This is also reflected in the need for escape, especially through drugs consumption, which essentially isolates people from society — both literally and metaphorically. In the business world, social concern for employees is giving way to increasingly self-centred corporations obsessed with personal gain.

Such trends will have manifestations in other areas, such as the retail and leisure industries. For example, people want to be different, and require customized and unique experiences. These kinds of movement are described by B. Joseph Pine and James Gilmore in their book *The Experience Economy* (1999). They propose that 'customers value experiences more highly than either goods or services'. As there is now little to choose between mass produced brands in terms of quality, just having an increasing variety of goods no longer satisfies customers' needs. Even the differentiating quality of good service is becoming taken for granted. This means that what makes a business different in the future will be giving customers engaging and memorable experiences that affect them personally. People already spend money on acquiring experiences – in theme parks, at Disneyworld, or speciality coffee shops. The experience of the Eden Project is more than just walking round a giant greenhouse learning about economic plants. It includes works of art that delight the senses, and live performers who entertain both musically and with stories about the plants.

Shopping malls will come to offer more than just goods for sale. Shop staff will be entertaining you with their patter (as in traditional open-air markets) or even with their juggling skills (as pizza chefs do), as shopping becomes more a theatrical and staged experience. Customers who enjoy this will stay around longer and spend more. This will also become true for websites and internet shopping. It is already happening with television and internet technology, which learn your preferences and then present you with programmes you like, and with information that you want to know.

Pine and Gilmore's thesis can be seen as a journey through the Four Realities and eventually leads to 'transformation'. From commodities (Unitary) and goods (Sensory), you pass through service provision (Social), towards mass customization and experiences (Mythic). Finally, in Fifth Position, people seek personal growth and transformation. For this they are willing to pay guides such as personal coaches and engage therapists of many kinds, to assist them in their quest. There are already TV programmes in which people are taught how to flirt, to date, to improve their financial situation – all thereby change their lifestyle, and, in the process, enhance their self-perception, confidence and self-esteem.

WHERE NEXT?

Spotting trends and following stories into the future will motivate you to begin further adventures. If you did not believe that, you would not bother to set outcomes! Continue to envision new goals, decide what you want to learn, who you want to be, and devise ways of achieving these things. In this way you will continue to transform yourself. And now, as with Rick and Louis, it's time to start that journey across the tarmac, trusting that all will be well.

ENVOI

No man ever steps in the same river twice, for it's not the same river and he's not the same man.

HERACLITUS

A book about change is a river you cannot step into twice; you will be different each time you read it. How have you changed since you last read these words? What have been the significant and transformative changes in your life, that have enabled you to become more flexible, more open, more aware in perceiving what is out there in the world?

Life will always be a balancing act between the divergent, expansive desire to innovate and explore, and the convergent, reflective need to create a stable reality in which you can be at home. The more you intervene in the world, the more you will learn from your experience, and the greater your expertise becomes in implementing change. However, this is not about adopting a superior attitude towards other people. Demonstrate your desire to learn by being curious and asking questions. Humility is essential. The more authentic you are, the more others will be inspired to follow your example. Treat the universe lightly, with a sense of humour. Laughter is often the outward sign of knowledge turning to wisdom.

Contact Information

The Author

Peter Young has the following website:
www.understandingnlp.com

and can be contacted by email:
peter.young10@virgin.net

The Eden Project

www.edenproject.com

Other books in this series

Coach, Steve Bavister and Amanda Vickers

Consultant, Anna Hipkiss

Entrepreneur, Alex McMillan

Leader, Catherine Doherty and John Thompson

Motivator, Frances Coombes

Presenter, Alan Mars

Team Player, Lesley Gosling

Bibliography

Acland, Andrew, *Resolving Disputes without going to Court: A Consumer Guide to Alternative Dispute Resolution*, London, Hutchinson Business Books, 1995.

Anderson, Dean and Anderson, Linda Ackerman, *Beyond Change Management: Advanced Strategies for Today's Transformational Leaders*, San Francisco, Jossey-Bass/Pfeiffer, 2001.

Bateson, Gregory, 'The Logical Categories of Learning and Communication' in *Steps to an Ecology of Mind: A Revolutionary Approach to Man's Understanding of Himself*, New York, Chandler Publishing Company, Ballantine Books, 1972.

Bronowski, Jacob, *The Ascent of Man*, London, British Broadcasting Corporation, 1973.

Burns, Sarah and Bulman, Chris, *Reflective Practice in Nursing: The Growth of the Professional Practitioner*, 2nd edition, Oxford, Blackwell Science, 2000.

Charvet, Shelle Rose, *Words that Change Minds: Mastering the Language of Influence*, 2nd edition, Dubuque, Kendall/Hunt Publishing Company, 1997.

de Bono, Edward, *Six Action Shoes*, London, HarperCollins Publishers, 1991.

de Geus, Arie, *The Living Company: Growth, Learning and Longevity in Business*, London, Nicholas Brealey Publishing, 1997.

Dyson, James, interviewed by Peter Day on 'In Business: The Moneymakers' broadcast on Radio 4 on 2 November 1998.

Dyson, James, interviewed by Libby Purves on 'Midweek' broadcast on BBC Radio 4 on 5 December 2001.

Egan, Kieran, *The Educated Mind: How Cognitive Tools Shape Our Understanding*, University of Chicago Press, 1997.

Gaskins, Bob, interviewed by Peter Day on 'In Business' broadcast on BBC Radio 4 on 7 February 2002.

Grint, Keith, *Fuzzy Management: Contemporary Ideas and Practices at Work*, Oxford University Press, 1997.

Hari, Johann, 'Forbidden Love' in *The Guardian*, 9 January 2002, pp. 8–9.

Harvey-Jones, John, *Making it Happen: Reflections on Leadership*, pp. 115–16, William Collins, 1988.

Bibliography

Lawson, Hilary, *Closure: A Story of Everything*, London, Routledge, 2001.

Levicki, Cyril, *Developing Leadership Genius: The Nature and Nurture of Leaders*, Maidenhead, McGraw-Hill, 2002.

Marshak, Robert J., 'Metaphors, Metaphoric Fields and Organizational Change', in David Grant and Cliff Oswick, eds, *Metaphors and Organizations*, London, Sage Publications, 1996.

McWhinney, Will, 'The Matter of Einstein Square Dancing with Magritte', *Cybernetics and Human Knowing*, Vol. 3, No. 3, 1995.

McWhinney, Will, *Paths of Change: Strategic Choices for Organizations and Society*, London, Sage Publications, 1997.

McWhinney, Will, Webber, James, Smith, Douglas and Novokowsky, Bernie, *Creating Paths of Change: Managing Issues and Resolving Problems in Organizations*, London, Sage Publications, 1997.

Norman, Marc and Stoppard, Tom, *Shakespeare in Love: A Screenplay*, London: Faber, 1999.

Pine, B. Joseph and Gilmore, James, *The Experience Economy: Work is Theatre and Every Business is a Stage*, Boston, Harvard Business School Press, 1999.

Putnam, Robert, *Bowling Alone: The Collapse and Revival of American Community*, New York, Simon & Schuster, 2000.

Rickards, Tudor, interviewed by Peter Day on 'In Business' broadcast on BBC Radio 4, January 2002.

Robbins, Harvey and Finley, Michael, *Why Change Doesn't Work: Why Initiatives Go Wrong and How to Try Again – And Succeed*, London, Texere Publishing, 1997.

Robbins, Harvey and Finley, Michael, *Why Teams Don't Work: What Went Wrong and How to Make It Right*, London, Texere Publishing, 2000.

Roberts, Monty, *Join-Up: Horse Sense for People*, London, HarperCollins Publishers, 2000.

Robinson, Graham, *Managing After the Superlatives: Effective Senior Management Development for the 1990s*, Wirral, Tudor Business Publishing Ltd, 1992.

Schwartz, Peter, *The Art of the Long View: Scenario Planning – Protecting Your Company Against an Uncertain World*, London, Century Business, 1991.

Senge, Peter, *The Fifth Discipline: The Art & Practice of the Learning Organization*, London, Century Business, 1990.

Bibliography

Sheth, Jagdish and Sisodia, Rajendra, 'The Seismic Impact of Technology', *Optimize*, February 2002.

Smit, Tim, 'A Passion that Consumes' *Plymouth Western Morning News* special edition 'Welcome to Eden' souvenir supplement to commemorate the opening of the Eden Project, p. 5, 2001a.

Smit, Tim, *Eden*, London, Bantam Press, Transworld Publishers, 2001b.

Sutherland, Stuart, *Irrationality: The Enemy Within*, London, Constable, 1992.

Szulanski, Gabriel and Winter, Sidney, 'Getting It Right the Second Time', *Harvard Business Review*, January 2002.

Vogler, Christopher, *The Writer's Journey: Mythic Structure for Storytellers and Screenwriters*, London, Pan Books, 1999 (2nd revised edition)

Young, Peter, *Understanding NLP: Metaphors and Patterns of Change*, Carmarthen, Crown House Publishing, 2001.

NOTES

NOTES